The Attachment Solution

To the three Js
– always with you

The Attachment Solution

Let Go of Your Fears and Learn How to Have Happier Relationships

Charisse Cooke

Copyright © Charisse Cooke 2024
Cover design by Anna Morrison

Sourcebooks and the colophon are registered trademarks of Sourcebooks.

This publication is designed to provide accurate and authoritative information
in regard to the subject matter covered. It is sold with the understanding
that the publisher is not engaged in rendering legal, accounting, or other
professional service. If legal advice or other expert assistance is required,
the services of a competent professional person should be sought. —*From
a Declaration of Principles Jointly Adopted by a Committee of the American
Bar Association and a Committee of Publishers and Associations*

Published by Sourcebooks
P.O. Box 4410, Naperville, Illinois 60567-4410
(630) 961-3900
sourcebooks.com

This edition originally published in 2024 in Great Britain by Vermilion, an imprint
of Ebury Publishing. Vermilion is part of the Penguin Random House group of
companies whose addresses can be found at global.penguinrandomhouse.com

Cataloging-in-Publication Data is on file with the Library of Congress.

Printed and bound in the United States of America.
POD

Contents

Everything we say and do
in a relationship
is a reaction
to love
or a lack of love

Introduction

When things are going well in our relationships, love comes very easily. We are patient and kind, we laugh effortlessly and forgive small missteps. We feel happy and confident within ourselves.

When things are not going well in our relationships, love becomes hard. We are intolerant, we are easily annoyed or become worried. We feel unhappy and are negative about ourselves or others.

The moment we perceive things to be 'going wrong', our instinct to protect and defend ourselves is much greater than our instinct to trust or feel optimistic. We can put all our efforts into fighting our partners, rather than communicating and problem-solving.

It is only when we become aware of our own overly protective, self-defeating behaviour that we can begin to exercise choice over what we do and behave in healthier and more constructive ways.

- Do you feel confused by what takes place in relationships?
- Do you rarely get your needs met by the people you love?
- Do you often feel disappointed by other people?
- Do you struggle to contain your emotions and either explode or withdraw?

- Do you want nothing more than to be loved and
  cared for?
- Do you wonder why having relationships is so hard
  for you?

If these resonate, from an attachment perspective, you
might be insecurely attached – either anxious, avoidant or a
combination of the two. You may have learnt that relationships can be a source of stress and difficulty, and you keep
experiencing the same pain cycles in your partnerships.

What Is Attachment Theory?

Pioneered in England in the 1950s, attachment theory was
developed by John Bowlby and Mary Ainsworth, who were
able to classify and predict how children would relate to
others and have relationships later in life based on the consistency of care they received from their caregivers when
they were infants. Since then, vast amounts of research and
countless studies have made attachment theory the definitive
basis for psychology and psychotherapy. Today, we understand that what happens in our adult romantic relationships
is neither random nor mysterious – it is highly predictable,
and the first step is understanding our own attachment
styles:

SECURE ATTACHMENT

When we have a secure attachment, we feel satisfied in our
relationships, trust our partners, and believe we are worthy
of love. We have pretty good self-esteem and hold our partners in high esteem too. We support our partners and our
partners support us. Communication is relatively easy and
fraught, volatile interactions do not happen frequently.

Insecure attachments

ANXIOUS ATTACHMENT

When we have an anxious attachment, we seldom feel satisfied in relationships. We struggle to trust and don't feel worthy of love. Our self-esteem can be low and yet we can idealise others (and then feel disappointed when they don't live up to our expectations). This is a high-anxiety way of relating that can include: over-functioning, ruminating, worrying, controlling and people-pleasing, and then becoming angry and ambivalent.

AVOIDANT ATTACHMENT

This falls into two categories:

- **Dismissive avoidant:** When we have a dismissive avoidant attachment, we do not feel satisfied in our relationships. We are dismissive and critical of our partners, and struggle with closeness or emotional intimacy. We trust ourselves but not others. We keep loved ones at arm's length as we need space and distance in relationships. This is a low-anxiety relating style that can include: under-functioning, defensiveness, hyper-independence, being rejecting, shutting down and withholding.
- **Fearful avoidant:** When we have a fearful avoidant attachment, we can struggle to feel satisfied in our relationships because we find them hugely stressful. We don't trust ourselves and don't believe we are worthy of love. This is a high-anxiety way of relating that can include: high-conflict arguing; having dramatic, addictive and dysfunctional relationships; impulsivity; ruminating and high stress as

relationships progress and intimacy is expected to develop.

When we're anxiously attached, we exhaust ourselves emoting; when we're dismissive avoidant we shut down and feel too little; and when we're in fearful avoidance we are out of control of our erratic feelings altogether. As we'll explore in this book, despite our natural need to love, attachment theory shows us that we have been profoundly impacted by our experiences from childhood and our previous relationships, and our need to protect ourselves has become greater than our need to love.

When it comes to our intimate relationships, we act from a place of fear. We're scared we will choose the wrong person. We're scared the person we are with doesn't love us enough. We're scared to get close. We're scared to be on our own. We're scared the one we love is pulling away. We're scared when someone seems really interested in us. It cannot be overstated how, when we love or try to be loved, our past permeates our present in the most all-consuming and powerful ways. This can make getting close to someone else, and staying close, very difficult.

We've never wanted more from each other in relationships than we do now and we've also never been more frightened of having those relationships. Because of this, I have come to understand great partnerships are the reward for incredibly brave people.

This book will show you how to let go of your fears and love without history.

Why This Book?

I discovered very early on in my 20-year career as a psychotherapist that all roads seem to lead to our relationships.

Relationships form the bedrock of our happiness for many of us, and when that bedrock develops cracks, it can destabilise us quickly and painfully.

I have learnt the merit of exploring things with clients, of helping them to understand their patterns and their behaviour, getting clear on the origins of their distress and the meaning it has for them. And I have also discovered that being able to offer some tools and guidance to clients, beyond just the intellectual understanding and awareness of the issues, goes a very long way. We want solutions to our relationship problems and rightly so: there is ample data that highlights that social relationships – especially romantic ones – have huge long-term effects on our well-being (for better or worse). Our intimate partnerships are intrinsic to our health and contentment.

I believe that love is something magical and indefinable, but I also believe that love is an action. There are many practicalities to love; there are ways of demonstrating it and there are ways of destroying it. In order to experience fulfilling partnerships, we need to understand as much of this as possible.

This book offers a wealth of solutions to our most pressing relationship problems and came about from a desire to distil everything I work on with my clients, everything I teach online, and everything I have learnt in my own personal life in one place. I believe this is the kind of book we all need. It will show you which attachment styles are relevant to you and will give you the strategies and tools you need for your relationships to thrive. It is a guide to help you develop the skills you need in your relationships, so you feel stronger, wiser and, most importantly, *equipped* to create truly extraordinary love stories.

How to Use This Book

This is not an academic book. This is a practical guide that will educate and inform, but mainly it will show you how to develop the skills you need to have more security and resilience in your romantic life – and in all other areas of your life too. When we are insecurely attached (this encompasses both anxious and avoidant), we behave in ways that are defensive. We can be extreme in our thinking and behaving, and this can have negative consequences on our relationships. We lack boundaries, we communicate in destructive ways and we can get stuck in negative loops of blame and resentment.

I recommend reading all the chapters on the various attachment styles in Part II, as you might recognise your thoughts and behaviour in them all. Though we often have a dominant relating style, we may also have different ways of relating that reflect other aspects of our personality or the sense of security we feel in certain dynamics with certain people. Our attachment style is not fixed; rather it is in constant flux, based on who we're with, what is happening within that relationship, the level of stress we're experiencing, and our ability to manage and maintain our emotions and responses. In our pursuit of being more secure, we need to bring our attention to the behaviours that are blocking us and understand the various ways we can behave – some of which may be anxious and some of which may be avoidant.

The book is set out in four parts: the origins of our attachments; the traits and tendencies of each attachment style; the solutions to becoming more relationally skilled/secure; and a deeper look at our insecure ways of relating, plus common relationship dynamics/traps within partnerships.

In Part I, we'll explore the history of your attachments, outlining the attachment styles and typical problems that relationships encounter as a result. A question I am asked frequently in my consulting room is: 'Why are relationships so hard?' The answer, of course, is that relationships are challenging and require more and more work as our lives become more and more complex in modern-day society. These chapters give you the tools to analyse what it is that is making relationships difficult for you, and the origins of the struggle, so you may develop understanding and insight into your relational style. We will look back over your childhood experiences, your school friendships and your entire romantic life. All of these will have shaped and informed your attachment blueprint.

In Part II, we'll look at the patterns that are generally evident in relationships. We will discover your attachment traits and tendencies, the power of these unconscious behaviours and the role they may play in your relational pain. By the end of this section, you will have a good overview of your relational patterns and how much distress and difficulty is being unconsciously perpetuated, and know exactly what to tackle in order to grow and have different kinds of relationships.

Part III is all about breaking those patterns and offering solutions. We'll explore how to be relational, how we can take appropriate responsibility in our lives, and how important it is for us to have insight into our own behaviour. We'll drill down into emotional regulation to understand exactly what this is and how we may self-soothe and also co-regulate with our partners. I'll ask you to challenge any distorted thinking you may be experiencing as part of your insecure attachment, because our insecurity is maintained through unhelpful cognitions and is therefore vital to address.

I've dedicated a whole chapter to communication: the mistakes we make when we argue, what healthy communication looks like, and the importance of communicating with respect and care. We'll also explore boundaries in this section, as insecure ways of relating are often boundaryless and not likely to help you or your partner feel safe. This offers a new, healthy way of protecting ourselves in our relationships that doesn't involve shutting down or pushing our partners away.

Part IV discusses all-important relationship dynamics. We'll look at relationship traps – such as the anxious avoidant dance, exploring why this dynamic can be so destructive and offering clear steps to tackle this in your relationships. We'll also explore the anxious anxious and avoidant avoidant partnerships, with advice and solutions on how to work on these unions and bring about greater fulfilment. This section concludes with looking at the secure insecure possibilities within relationships and how, if we have an understanding of our insecure ways of relating, any relationship is able to prosper. It also asks when we need to stay in a relationship and when we need to walk away.

At the end of each chapter, I've provided some journalling prompts for you. Journalling is a writing exercise that offers us an opportunity to dedicate time to certain topics in a deeper, more considered way. We can scratch beneath the surface and explore our thoughts and feelings about subjects that matter to us. We can bring curiosity and openness to our inner lives and often arrive at a new understanding of ourselves. Writing can unlock memories and emotions of which we were unaware, which can help us learn about ourselves and what we need. I recommend having a pen and paper beside you as you work through the book, journalling in private and bringing compassion and courage to the work. Journalling exercises are about reflection, not judgement or finding fault.

While this is a book predominantly about romantic adult attachments, our relating styles are relevant to all the relationships of our life, so you can keep that in mind as you read through the chapters. They may shed some light on your relationships with your friends, colleagues, siblings and the wider community. I have also tried to keep my descriptions of relationships generic and broad so they can apply to you whether you are single, dating, in a serious, long-term relationship, married, divorced or breaking up. Our attachment insecurities are evident at different times and these ways of relating will be relevant wherever you are on your relationship journey.

I also want this book to be as inclusive as possible. The ideas, tools and themes outlined here are applicable to all romantic relationships and move across race, sex, sexuality, gender and culture. Attachment is a vast subject, and deeply complex, and I have purposely extrapolated what I believe to be the most important ideas around adult attachment so we may apply them to our equally complex lives and relationships. Due to this, I have not been able to explore the nuance of the many facets of relationships. This book is for and about all human interactions, and I hope you will be able to see yourself within its pages, take what is useful to you and leave the rest.

Let's Get Started

Worrying about or feeling unhappy in our relationships is not where we should be targeting our efforts. We should be putting our energy into new behaviour – behaviour that might challenge the status quo, shake things up or stretch us, and help us to develop our self-esteem and relational skills.

This is not about becoming different people or trying to be perfect; it's about stepping up in our relationships, being versions of ourselves we want to be, and then seeing what kind of a relationship is on offer with the people we are with, and whether that is right for us. It's about giving our relationships a proper chance. Whatever happens, we are rewarded. We are rewarded with the peace of mind of knowing we did all we could in our partnerships to truly explore what was possible, and with the knowledge that we have grown as a person.

This book is about deeply and thoroughly exploring the nature of your insecure behaviours, thought processes, attitudes and ways of relating, so you know exactly what to focus on, and then supplying you with tools and strategies to break those patterns once and for all. This allows you to be accountable to yourself and to avoid these pitfalls in the future. As you create new behaviours and better habits, you create the secure and fulfilling relationships you deserve. I'm looking forward to walking this road less travelled with you.

PART I

Why Relationships Are So Hard

There are many reasons we find relationships hard and to make sense of this, in this section we'll explore the history of your attachments, outlining the attachment styles and typical problems that relationships encounter as a result. These chapters analyse what is making partnerships challenging for you, so you may develop an understanding and insight into your relational style, and the specific behaviours that you can work on to create more harmony and ease in your personal life.

CHAPTER 1

Understanding Your Attachment Style

What if I told you that everything that is happening in your relationship right now was inevitable? What if the pain you've experienced and the heartbreak you've endured were not only highly likely but to be expected?

I have sat with hundreds of clients and watched them choose the very things they didn't want: unavailable people, people with financial issues, people who don't like sex, workaholics, underachievers and under-earners, addicts and alcoholics, people who aren't 'strong enough' or those who are controlling. In our rational minds, we all know we want kind, decent people who we can have fun with, will support us and who we are attracted to. And yet, contrary to what we might believe, we don't choose what we want in relationships; we choose what's familiar. As you'll come to see, our rational minds have nothing to do with who and how we love.

Love Is Learnt

A common question I ask my clients is 'Who taught you that?' or 'Where did you learn that?', because a huge amount of how we think and behave is learnt behaviour from long ago. Our greatest and most efficacious teachers are our parents, caregivers, family, teachers, friends and partners. From them we learn how important we are, how interested people are in what we have to share, how enchanted others are by us (or not), how either smart or behind we are at school and then work, what it takes to get affirmation and validation from those most important to us, and what it feels like when we don't get any of that.

Everything we believe, every thought we have, every fearful insecurity, every anxious worry, negative assumption, unhelpful judgement – none of it is new. It's old. It's as old as you are. It's a unique amalgam of all the experiences that you've had, how you've made sense of them, and how they have formed a comprehensive belief system about yourself, other people and the world. They are the lessons you've learnt, and you live and love accordingly.

We have absolutely no say over our very first, and most influential, love affair: the one we have with our parents/caregivers. How they showed up for us will imprint in our attachment systems not only what to expect and what we deserve, but what we will find *attractive*. And all of it is unconscious.

'So Jay has gone quiet. Again.'

My client, Maud, is sighing as she recounts the latest in her dating life. Since I've been working with her, she has dated three men. Each time, there has been a lot of initial interest, messaging late into the night, some fun first dates and good sex. But after a few weeks or months, they disappear abruptly.

'Hmmm,' I say. 'These men seem to have a lot in common.'

'In common? They're all completely different!' Maud exclaims.

'What I mean is, this is sounding like a pattern,' I elaborate. 'They appear available at the beginning but then prove to be very much unavailable.' Maud shrugs. 'I think you are unconsciously choosing men who are unavailable,' I continue. 'With your history, you've learnt that men don't stick around.'

'What? How is a man not sticking around familiar to me?' Maud looks confused. We sit in silence for a while. Eventually, I crack.

'Your father . . .' I say.

What we do in our relationships today was taught through the relationships we had with our caregivers when we were young, the relationships that were modelled to us, and what we experienced in our relationships growing up and in adulthood.

Maud's father left her and her mother when she was just a baby, and she'd only see him occasionally. Sadly, this left Maud expecting men not to prioritise her, not to be around much and to be inconsistent. When she did see her father, it would be thrilling and fun – intense reunions of laughter, hugging and some small gift she would cherish. He was tall and strong and would swing her around in the air; Maud told me how exhilarating it felt whenever she saw him. This is her pattern, what is familiar to her. Maud's adult relationships and the men she attracts and finds attractive reinforce this pattern, and I suspect she doesn't believe she deserves someone to wholeheartedly commit to her.

This is what humans do. We recreate what is familiar. Familiarity is better than the unknown, even if what is familiar is painful. I'm sure if we had explored Maud's father's history there would have been childhood abandonment for him, too. And this, tragically, is how the cycles are passed down from generation to generation.

We all have our own version of this: experiences (both positive and negative) we had growing up that taught us what love is, how it feels and what people who love us do (or don't do). We soak it all up and will unconsciously seek out people who will evoke the same feelings and outcomes. We need to become aware of any unhelpful experiences we had, lessons we learnt growing up and then later in our lives in our adult relationships, and how those are impacting our ability to give and receive love today. Attachment theory can teach us a lot about how we relate and why.

The Lasting Impact of Our Early Attachments

Attachment theory provides an internal working model for how we will have relationships throughout our lives. Also known as our relating style, our attachment will influence who we choose, how we will interact with those people, and what behaviour we might evoke from them. Our childhood relationships provide a prototype for all our future relationships and how we will experience them, so it's very useful to explore what we learnt – both helpful and unhelpful.

From the moment we are conceived, we are learning what to expect from life:

- Are the people surrounding us calm and healthy?
- Are they available and able to meet our needs?
- Is the environment safe and stable?
- Are our parents/caregivers loving to each other?

These factors inundate our young, forming brains and nervous systems with information that will shape our lives forever.

Secure attachment

If we had parents/caregivers who were consistent with us, who were able to reliably comfort and soothe us while managing their own stress, we learnt that we are protected and can rely on others. If our home environment had a sense of stability and the people in it were cared for and respected, we learnt that the world is a safe place and we developed a sense of belonging. This safety helped us build a foundation of trust, both in ourselves and others, and we have a confident, positive outlook on life. We developed a healthy, easy bond with our parents/caregivers, feeling sure of their love for us and finding solace in their presence. Emotionally, we were acknowledged and validated by our caregivers. We developed the ability to accurately identify our emotions and, in time, learnt to control these emotions and not be impulsive or instantly gratified. We had sufficiently good-enough parents/caregivers and developed secure attachment.

Anxious attachment

If we had parents/caregivers who were unreliable and inconsistent, we learnt that we can't always rely on people being there when we need them. Rather than developing trust, our working model was imprinted with a sense of uncertainty about whether our carers were able to love us. Because of the inconsistency of the care, we felt insecure and developed the belief that we are unlovable. We struggled to form emotional bonds with our parents/caregivers and, because of that, we struggled to feel safe in the world. We learnt that people will not automatically meet our needs and so became preoccupied with our parents'/caregivers' availability and monitored their responsiveness to us. We felt conflicted because we wanted to be close to them but were also ambivalent about whether we should get close, because we might be let down. As our anxiety became more entrenched, we struggled to manage our emotions and often felt overwhelmed by them. Due to unreliable parenting, our attachments were sources of stress rather than comfort, and we developed anxious attachment.

Avoidant attachment

If we had parents/caregivers who were unresponsive to us, who could not comfort us when we were upset or crying, and who actively discouraged us from showing emotion, we learnt that our needs will not be met with warmth or acceptance. We did not develop trust in other people; instead, we learnt to trust only ourselves and eventually refused help or emotional support from others. Because our parents/caregivers sometimes showed annoyance when we were experiencing a problem, we learnt that closeness with other people can be hurtful. We learnt not to associate security with others and could feel suffocated when people tried to get too close. Because our feelings were invalidated, we stopped showing or experiencing our emotions too. Our emotional development stalled. Lacking affection and physical touch, in time, we developed a discomfort with physical closeness and avoided eye contact. We learnt it is safer and easier to be separate from other people, so began valuing our independence and freedom. We stopped relying on other people and didn't like other people relying on us. We developed an avoidant attachment as we learnt attachments are too disappointing and are therefore best avoided.

Within avoidance, there are two categories:

DISMISSIVE AVOIDANT ATTACHMENT

If our parents/caregivers were very unavailable or rejecting when we were an infant or a child, if they were not able to consistently and predictably meet our needs, over time we learnt that our caregivers were not reliable and our emotional needs would not be met by others. We learnt that we needed to distance ourselves emotionally from them and that we had to self-soothe on our own. Because of this, we disconnected from our emotional selves, developing avoidance of closeness and intimacy as a way of staying safe.

Our caregivers may have been absent to us due to their own issues, like depression or anxiety, and we came to the conclusion we needed to do life on our own. In order to survive, we stamped out feelings of our own uncertainty and powerlessness, instead believing that it was our caregivers who were uncertain and lacking in power as parents. We felt rejected and we learnt rejection, internalising the process, and soon began rejecting those around us. Relying only on ourselves seemed the best course of action. We didn't like people wanting things from us and, because of our emotional numbing out, we thought that people with needs were weak. Attachments were a source of disappointment and felt rejecting, so we ourselves became rejecting and developed dismissive avoidant attachment.

FEARFUL AVOIDANT ATTACHMENT

If our parents/caregivers exhibited unpredictable or contrasting ways of behaving and were not able to consistently comfort us – for example, they could be warm and loving one moment, and then angry and punishing the next – we developed a sense of fear towards them. If the home environment was unstable or chaotic and we experienced neglect, trauma or abuse, we learnt that our caregivers were unable to meet our needs and instead we experienced pain and abandonment. We began to have high anxiety and high avoidance in our view of our relationships, as we tried to keep ourselves safe – something that was very difficult due to our parents'/caregivers' unpredictability and sometimes frightening behaviour. Because the people around us struggled to manage their own emotions, we did not learn to manage our own, and were often plagued with self-doubt and worry. If our parents/caregivers were overly strict or dismissive of our feelings, this reinforced the idea that the best thing to do is withdraw from connection as a way of protecting ourselves. Even though we really wanted love and care, it felt too dangerous to stay close to our parents/caregivers. Our attachments were a huge source of fear which made avoiding closeness a necessity, and we developed fearful avoidant attachment.

You may recognise some or all of these in yourself. From an attachment perspective, many of us relate in insecurely attached ways, and being raised by fallible human beings, with their own attachment wounding, combined with the circumstances of our family and life in general when we were born and growing up, leaves a lot of room for many lessons to be learnt. It's useful to reflect on this to understand just how complex our attachment wiring has been.

Attachment in Adult Relationships

Either anxious, avoidant or a combination of the two, our adult attachment responses will reveal what our fears are in relationships, and how we try to get our needs met and protect ourselves, especially when stressed or experiencing difficulty.

Secure attachment

When we are securely attached, we feel satisfied in our adult relationships. We feel confident and trusting in ourselves and our partners, and enjoy plenty of independence. When secure, we offer comfort when our partners feel distressed and we also go to our partners for support or help when we need it. The relationship tends to be drama-free and honest, and has open and easy communication and ways of dealing with conflict. We are loving and respectful towards each other.

Anxious attachment

When we are anxiously attached, we are dissatisfied in our relationships. We can be preoccupied with what is missing in the relationship and focus on our partners' failings or limitations. We're generally always seeking a sense of connection from our partners, which we do by protesting, nagging or controlling. Thinking about our relationship (which we do a lot) can be a significant source of stress (high anxiety). We feel deeply saddened and believe we are not getting enough love. We are fearful of rejection and can become jealous, suspicious, demanding or possessive. We can also over-function in the relationship, doing the majority of the emotional labour, being over-accommodating, people-pleasing and contorting ourselves to appease our partners.

Avoidant attachment

When we are avoidantly attached, we emotionally distance ourselves from our partners. We seek isolation despite our human need for connection. We go inward, denying the importance of loved ones and detaching easily from them. We can be quite defensive and have the ability to shut down emotionally. Even in heated or emotional situations, we are able to turn off our feelings and not react.

DISMISSIVE AVOIDANT ATTACHMENT

We create distance by being grandiose and critical at times, often numbed out from our feelings (low anxiety). We can be guarded and evasive, and dodge and lose interest very quickly when confronted with the responsibilities of a relationship. Generally, relationships are seen as unneeded, as we believe we are 'fine as we are' and we value independence over intimacy. We can stonewall and withdraw from partners, as closeness can feel suffocating.

FEARFUL AVOIDANT ATTACHMENT

Having the characteristics of both anxious and avoidant attachments, we desire close relationships but feel uncomfortable relying on others and fear being rejected. We deeply want relationships but can get extremely fearful when things progress and closeness and intimacy are increasing. We may end relationships abruptly (high anxiety). We can have high-conflict or addictive relationships as we are accustomed to chaotic emotional interactions. We can feel stuck in our lives and relationships.

The diagram below shows how our childhood experiences shape our attitudes, beliefs and behaviour within adult relationships.

Childhood attachment	Adult attachment
SECURE	**SECURE**
• Learns to trust caregivers' presence and consistency • Has warm relationship with caregivers	• Comfortable and relaxed in relationships • Able to seek support from partner

Childhood attachment	Adult attachment
ANXIOUS	**ANXIOUS**
• Learns parents are inconsistent and not always available, becomes hypervigilant to their presence • Anxious about caregivers	• Fears rejection from partners and others • Needs to maintain closeness at all times in order to feel connected and safe
AVOIDANT	**AVOIDANT**
• Learns caregivers are unreliable and develops mistrust • Retreats into self	• Has a greater sense of autonomy in relationships • Tends to shut themselves off emotionally
DISMISSIVE AVOIDANT	**DISMISSIVE AVOIDANT**
• Experiences inconsistency and rejection from caregivers, develops mistrust • Relies on self	• Rejecting of others in order to stay safe • Highly autonomous in relationships
FEARFUL AVOIDANT	**FEARFUL AVOIDANT**
• Experiences inconsistency and rejection from caregivers, develops fear and mistrust • Withdraws from closeness with others for own safety	• Highly anxious and fearful of being in a relationship and of being alone • Either avoids relationships or has emotionally unavailable relationships

Love hurts

When our insecure attachment has been activated, the key feature of our relationships is a real or perceived lack of safety. This is shown by fear being a core component and driver of our behaviours. What else could be behind the anxious need for reassurance or the avoidant process of distance and control? It is a sad truth that the very things we do in an effort to maintain safety – the anxious or avoidant coping strategies – are exactly what maintain our lack of safety and perpetuate the problem.

Uncovering Your Attachment Style

Look through the tick lists on the next couple of pages to discover which of the attachment style key traits and behaviours might be relevant to you. You will probably tick traits from more than one style, as our behaviour often embodies many different ways of relating. This will begin to highlight where you can focus your efforts to develop new ways of relating that will bring more security and happiness. We are able to replace old ways of thinking and learn new, affirming ways of thinking and behaving, rooted in love and hope.

We have the capacity to change how we relate.

It is useful to think about these traits with a specific relationship in mind, especially during times of stress. Go through the lists as many times as you like, each time thinking about a different relationship or circumstance of the relationship. Keep in mind that these statements can exist in mild, moderate and extreme ways. Tick any that are relevant to you.

If you are doing this with your partner, fill in the list together, getting each other's perspective on your behaviour and ways of relating.

Secure attachment

- I consider myself to be very emotionally available to others, but it can take me time to trust and share important things about myself.
- I don't get carried away or overwhelmed with emotions at the start of a relationship.
- I can read other people, assessing their intentions and if they are safe for me.
- I can tell if someone else is not interested in me or in having a relationship and can let them go.
- I feel comfortable having difficult conversations and working through issues in a relationship.
- I can communicate my feelings and needs to loved ones.
- I think I am good at compromise and communication.
- I believe I am worthy of love.
- If my partner upsets me, I feel comfortable sharing with them how I feel and I'm curious about what has caused them to behave like that.
- I am comfortable setting boundaries.
- Being vulnerable for me is not a big deal.
- Being affectionate with my partner is easy for me.
- I can adapt easily from being with my partner to being on my own.
- If my partner and I disagree I feel comfortable talking things through, apologising if necessary and making a repair.
- I am open to, and want to meet, my partner's needs.

- I look fondly at my partner and enjoy being with them.
- I can respect my partner's boundaries.
- I feel relaxed in my relationship.
- I believe that people are fundamentally good.
- When relationships end, I feel extremely sad and grieve but I am able to move on.

Anxious attachment

- I can idealise some people, putting them on a pedestal.
- If I sense a temperature change in my relationship, I feel panicky.
- I don't set boundaries until I am really angry and then I can punish or push people away.
- I am very aware of what other people need and put their needs ahead of my own. This can cause me to get resentful.
- I can fall in love easily.
- When hurt, I can be ambivalent about my partner getting close again. I want to connect with them but I also want to punish them for hurting me.
- I don't like being single. I'm actually quite scared of being alone.
- I am deeply impacted by rejection and abandonment.
- I find it hard to say no.
- I struggle to trust partners and can spend a lot of time reassurance-seeking.
- I sometimes have sex just to feel reassured or to get my partner's attention.
- It's hard for me to feel satisfied and connected in my relationships.
- I can get stuck in people-pleasing and catering to others, or complaining, criticising and/or venting.

- I expect people to be unavailable to me; I have negative expectations of others.
- Sometimes I can get enmeshed with my partners.
- I overthink, agonising over things I've said or done.
- I can be drawn to avoidant or unavailable people, or those who need rescuing.
- I can have surges of jealousy and/or anger.
- I struggle with self-esteem issues and low self-worth.
- If a relationship or casual fling doesn't work out, I can be bitter and resentful.

Avoidant attachment

- I can get upset when I don't get the space or time alone that I need.
- I sometimes don't know what I'm feeling.
- I don't like making plans in advance as it results in me feeling trapped.
- I'm not a talker. I don't like calling and messaging a lot.
- I don't fall in love easily.
- I am very independent; I like being alone and I struggle to ask for help.
- I can have emotion-free sex.
- I can physically or emotionally leave difficult conversations or situations.
- I can feel very stressed when my partner approaches me wanting to connect.
- I like to think things through in my head rather than talk things out.
- Sometimes I prefer casual sex instead of sex in a committed relationship.
- I don't believe relationships should need to be worked on.
- Taking responsibility in relationships is tiresome.
- I don't really understand what being vulnerable means.

- I can use fantasy or pornography as a substitute for sex.
- I'm not very tactile. Affection, cuddling and touch in general feels awkward and is unwanted.
- Being interested in personal growth and keeping the focus on my own issues is difficult for me.
- I sometimes do not remember my previous relationships or childhood.
- Maintaining eye contact is not easy for me.
- I take time to recover from relational conflict.

Dismissive avoidant attachment

- I don't need other people and wish others were less needy.
- I don't like other people invading my space.
- I can be judgemental of my partners and other people.
- Serious or long conversations are boring and unnecessary.
- It's challenging for me to be enthusiastic, encouraging and kind to my partner.
- I will progress relationships only when I'm ready.
- My partners complain I am controlling.
- I can be rude or unkind to partners, claiming it's being honest.
- When someone annoys me, I can quickly go off them.
- I can flip a switch and turn off my feelings.
- I am okay with who I am.
- Partners often want more from me.
- I'm not bothered by what others think of me.
- I am often late or cancel last minute.
- I prefer having my own space until I'm ready to connect.
- I don't consider close relationships to be hugely important.

- I can get stuck in arguing and insulting my partner, or leaving/stonewalling.
- I often think negatively about my partner, their behaviour and their character.
- I can blame my partner for most of the issues in our relationship.
- When relationships end, I can feel liberated.

Fearful avoidant attachment

- I find relationships very challenging and troubling – they create a lot of inner turmoil for me which I struggle to contain.
- My feelings in a relationship can be very up and down. It's either love or hate.
- As much as I want to be close to my partner, it can sometimes feel really difficult for me to allow it.
- My fear of rejection and abandonment drives most of my behaviour.
- As much as I want a close loving relationship, I am also terrified of having or losing a relationship.
- I can feel overwhelmed by my problems and implode or explode.
- After anxiously wanting to see my partner again, when with them I end up picking fights.
- My self-esteem is quite low.
- I can end relationships abruptly.
- I can escalate conversations and disagreements into unnecessary and extreme conflict.
- Even though my partner is expressive and loving, I struggle to accept it.
- I desire closeness with my partner but I can also feel angry with them at the same time.
- I want closeness but I'm also afraid of closeness. This can make me feel stuck.

- Whenever there is difficulty in a relationship, my first impulse is to break up.
- Sometimes I can get enmeshed with my partners, having addictive, dysfunctional or extreme relationships.
- Feeling safe in a relationship is not easy for me.
- I often yearn for people who I believe I am not worthy of.
- When a relationship ends I can feel very happy for a while but then become extremely depressed or low.
- As intimacy with my partner develops I can become frightened.
- I catastrophise and expect the worst-case scenario.

How we attach is on a continuum

We all attach in all of the ways described above. How we are attaching at any given moment is about how *safe* we are feeling in that environment or interaction. It's important to understand that each relationship we have is different and will evoke different relational responses in us. And even within relationships, different circumstances will evoke different reactions that we need to manage with love and care. We might be anxious with our partners, secure with our best friends, and utterly avoidant with our siblings. Or during an argument, we might start off anxious and then finish avoidant. The way we attach is fluid. Depending on our sense of safety, how we relate can include all these different ways of attaching. This is simply our biology; it is the human condition.

These reflections can really help us understand

ourselves and each other better. If we're feeling hurt because our partners are stepping away from us and withdrawing, we can remember that we ourselves do that in certain circumstances and perhaps we don't need to take it quite so personally. Likewise, we can identify the pain of feeling unsure and anxious in a relationship, so when we recognise that struggle in our partners, we can be more reassuring and supportive. Yes, we may have a dominant attachment style that we exhibit in many areas of our lives; however, our attachment fluctuates and is impacted by our mood, our interactions, stress and the state of the nation within our relationships. How we relate is dependent on the relationships we have and the changing nature of ourselves and others.

Attachment theory for modern love stories has to include knowledge of all attachment possibilities, so we can recognise what to work on and where to focus our efforts, if our aim is to be more secure and more satisfied, even in times of vulnerability or hurt. The exercise above has probably uncovered a lot of behaviour you were aware of and some you weren't. It's imperative we know the combination of traits that is unique to us so we can direct our self-work to these areas. Anxious and avoidant attachment can have us spinning our wheels doing the same unhelpful behaviours over and over. Taking a step back and looking at our ways of thinking and relating that are at the root of our insecure attachments shows us the way forward. Throughout this book you'll learn tools and skills to develop ways of being more relational and, therefore, improve your relationships and experience of love.

How we view ourselves and others from an attachment perspective

- Secure individuals have a positive view of themselves and a positive view of others (low anxiety), and experience a general comfort with closeness and can trust others with ease.
- Anxious individuals have a negative view of themselves and a positive view of others (high anxiety), and have a strong need for emotional closeness and a strong concern about being rejected.
- Dismissive avoidants have a positive view of themselves and a negative view of others (low anxiety), and view total independence and self-reliance as more important than intimacy.
- Fearful avoidants have a negative view of themselves and others (high anxiety), and avoid relationships for fear of rejection.

Relationship Problems

When we complain of being ignored, not listened to, neglected, disconnected and unsatisfied in our relationships, chances are we are coming from an **anxiously attached** position, which is generally categorised by wanting more: more time, more talking, more closeness, more attention, more effort. The wound these are touching is the yearning wound from long ago when there was inconsistency, lack, deprivation or neglect.

When we complain of feeling criticised or that whatever we do is never enough, when we want space and are confused 'what the problem is', the chances are we are **dismissively avoidant** in that moment, and this can be categorised by wanting less: less pressure, fewer 'demands', less physical touch and proximity, fewer people. The wound these are touching is when we felt a lack of warmth growing up, being criticised, rejected, suffocated or overwhelmed by others' emotions or needs as we became parentified (see more on this in Chapter 2) and had to care for others or were left to fend for ourselves.

And when we complain of all of the above and more, this is when we are experiencing a mixture of anxious and avoidant attachment fears, categorised as a **fearful avoidant** relating style, when we are scared to get close but also scared to be on our own. We might like the excitement of the beginning of a relationship but when it comes to genuinely getting close to someone, intimacy or responsibility, that's a pass. The wound these are touching is the terror relationships used to represent to us, when our environment was scary and dysfunctional and the people in it unreliable and struggling with their own issues.

These behaviours will suck the love out of any relationship, possibly lead to another ending, most likely reinforce our negative beliefs, and contribute to us feeling even less hopeful and open to the next relationship. It can be a vicious cycle, and one we need to thoroughly explore because what we are doing in our partnerships is not helping us to get anywhere near the fulfilling relationships we deserve. The research speaks very clearly: our attachment styles and their attendant behaviours are self-perpetuating. If nothing changes, nothing changes.

When working on our relationships, we can spend too much time talking about the conflict. We spend too much time analysing the problem or who is right and who's wrong. While these are important points, ultimately what needs to be worked on is how to grow within the relationship. All patterns present themselves every day in all manner of incarnations. It's not helpful to focus on the specific examples or their many manifestations; rather, we need to try and understand the process and symbolism behind the behaviour. The growth required in relationships is about bringing compassion to one another and pushing ourselves out of our comfort zones. This is where our energy needs to be directed, and this is what chapters 6–10 will clearly show you.

Understanding our attachment styles in action helps us to recognise what is playing out for us and when. The better we know ourselves and the people we care about, the better our mutual understanding, the better our ability to love one another.

You can prevent these pitfalls, create new behaviours and better habits, and achieve the secure, fulfilling relationship you desire. This book is about shifting away from insecure extremes so we can experience more security in our intimate lives.

Living the Dream: When We Feel Securely Attached

Attachment researchers talk about the 'secure base'. This ideally would have been a home environment, that supplied the security we needed to allow appropriate growth and development. It was a place where, more than anything else, we were safe. A place of rest, a place of calm, a place of security.

So, our homes and what took place in them was extremely important and remains crucial in our adulthood too. We do best if our homes are safe havens, if they offer us, our partners and our families all the security and love in the world.

From a secure base we can go out into the world and accomplish things, meet our goals, fulfil our potential, have fun and feel confident.

When our homes are not sanctuaries – when they are places of supreme loneliness, unpredictability, threat and lack of safety – we do not thrive; instead, we have to survive. When there is neglect, fighting, drinking and drugging, uncertainty, and any kind of atmosphere or behaviour that disrupts the peace in an ongoing and unhealthy way, we are nowhere near secure.

Therefore, our choice is imperative. Who we choose, the lifestyle that we are likely to lead with those people, the attitudes and behaviour of those we decide to have in our lives, is going to profoundly impact the quality of our lives.

Our work now is creating a safe relationship.

When we look around at our lives, when we're questioning what is right for us, when we think about the people we invite into our homes and bedrooms, it's useful to consider what we want, what love *really* is. We want to be able to say 'my safe place is you'.

Journalling prompts

- What have you discovered about how you relate to others and your attachment style?
- Did you mark traits and behaviours from more than one attachment style? It's useful to understand that our ways of relating are changeable and dependent on who we're with and what is happening in the moment, particularly stress and fear.

- Were you surprised by any traits that you recognised in yourself?
- What can you now notice about your behaviour when your insecure attachment is triggered? Do you people-please or defend?
- Are there particular traits you recognise that you really want to change because they cause you pain or problems?

CHAPTER 2

How Our Patterns Are Formed

A relational blueprint is created in the same way our attachment styles develop. Our relationships, experiences, environment and the reactions we have to all of those from birth onwards create the lens through which we will view every future interaction, experience and relationship. Our blueprint consolidates all that into patterns that our brain can comprehend and assimilate. Once created, we will automate those patterns – they become highly unconscious and we will perpetuate them moving forward. In this way, our past lives on in us today more than we realise, particularly in what we believe about others and the world, what we can expect, and what we deserve. It all comes together to form our blueprint and, if we're not careful, our destiny.

Many of our tender spots are tender because of repeated hurt or disappointment. These are things that we're very familiar with and will therefore react sensitively to when reminded of them in any way. When we are getting emotional, it's useful to slow things down and ask ourselves, 'How old do I feel right now?' This is not to point out how childish we are being, it's about ascertaining how old the hurt is. Because sometimes, the greater our reactions, the greater the likelihood we're touching something deeper and older.

Remembering the origin of our hurt helps us to see what we are experiencing in the present day with a bit more perspective and compassion. Many times, the yearning we are feeling in our relationship today is the same yearning we've had for most of our life: to be loved, acknowledged and adored by the people most important to us.

Childhood Experiences

We have been profoundly impacted by our experiences from childhood and our previous relationships, and these experiences shape us in every imaginable way; they're called our formative years for a reason. There are so many things to consider when exploring our past:

- What might have been happening for your parents/ caregivers when you were conceived and born.
- Whether there are mental health issues, diagnosed or not, in the family.
- Whether there was addiction (drug or alcohol abuse, or other addictions such as food, gambling or sex).
- Whether your parents/caregivers experienced trauma in their lives/childhoods.
- Whether your parents/caregivers may have experienced postpartum depression, psychosis or anxiety.
- The financial situation you were born into and the impact of that.
- Issues of class, discrimination, socio-economic status, inequities and adverse experiences of power, privilege and control.
- Whether you and your family experienced structural racism and the profound impact of prejudice and discrimination.

- Family roles (see overleaf). Often there are unspoken roles assigned to each child in a family which we take on to be our life roles.
- Disability – yours or other family members' and the impact of that.
- Whether you or any of your family were adopted or put up for adoption.
- Death (including miscarriages) can impact the home environment powerfully and for many years.
- Harassment, assault and rape are sadly very common and have a lasting effect, whether spoken about or not.
- Self-injury, suicidal thoughts and attempts can be secrets families carry.
- Whether you, or anyone you know, were refugees and asylum seekers. Themes of trauma, belonging and safety will be an ongoing legacy.
- Whether a parent, caregiver or family member went to prison. This creates absent family figures and can also contribute to a sense of shame or distrust.
- Domestic violence is a reality for many families and can have major ramifications.
- Whether there was divorce. How was it handled? How did you feel? What did you witness and learn about relationships from this?
- If there was child abuse, neglect, emotional, sexual or physical abuse or incest.
- Whether your sexuality was able to develop freely. Whether there were open, supportive discussions about sex, gender, identity and sexual development.
- Traumatising events and discrimination are part of our divided world. Have you been supported, represented and heard?
- Feelings of inferiority and powerlessness due to social ostracism.

- Whether you had experience of, or witnessed, bullying. This can take many forms and impacts multiple people in many ways.
- Baggage we inherit from our parents'/caregivers' childhood and their relationships. In what ways have your parents'/caregivers' issues been a part of your life and development?

These are just some examples of the very difficult, stressful and often traumatic life events or situations – which could be one-off events or ongoing issues – that have informed our sense of safety, trust and security, and will increase the likelihood of troubled relationships.

Family roles

Originally developed by Sharon Wegscheider-Cruse to identify dysfunctional family roles in alcoholic families, the idea of family members adapting to their environments and taking on specific, unspoken roles has been widely accepted to apply to complicated families in general, not just those with addiction. These established roles within our families can be highly unhealthy if they become fixed and we are punished for not fulfilling our role. These are unacknowledged and highly unconscious processes, and we can very easily take these roles with us into adulthood, because once we are accustomed to playing a role, it becomes internalised.

Have a look below and see if you can identify with any of these roles. Bear in mind that we can have more than one, or sometimes swap roles at different times:

HERO/GOLDEN CHILD

The hero is often considered 'the favourite child'. They are often an overachiever and represent success. They make the family look good. As an adult, the golden child can struggle with perfectionism and feel a lot of pressure. They might enjoy feeling special and being in the limelight; however, always being golden can come at a high personal cost.

SCAPEGOAT/TROUBLE-MAKER

This is the opposite of the golden child, where a child becomes 'the problem' in the family. They often act out with alcohol or drugs, develop mental health issues and generally draw negative attention to themselves and the family. Or it may not be particularly dramatic – the scapegoat might just be different and not fit in with what the family feels is best. They can be ostracised and isolated, and, rather than looking at any other problems within the family, everyone becomes over-focused on the scapegoat. These issues of not fitting in and being 'difficult' can haunt a scapegoat well into adulthood.

THE LOST CHILD

Because of all the positive attention the golden child receives and the negative attention the scapegoat gets, there is precious little left over, so the other child or children become forgotten or lost. Sometimes this happens in families where another sibling has a mental health issue or disability, or because the family is particularly large. The lost child can feel very lonely and craves attention, but feels they don't deserve it. They are self-sufficient and take care of themselves, trying not to be a bother to others. As an adult, they will struggle with asking for help and can be a loner or reclusive.

PEACEMAKER/MEDIATOR

The peacemaker tries to make everything okay in the family. As a child, they can try to mediate between parents/caregivers, putting all their needs aside to focus on the other people around them who are 'more important'. As an adult, the peacemaker is very tuned in to what other people are experiencing and will prioritise other people's needs over their own.

MASCOT/CLOWN

The family can rely on the mascot lightening the mood and making people laugh when things get too tense or serious at home. By bringing humour to situations, they can diminish real problems, while also getting whatever attention they can. Never taken seriously, the mascot can continue this into adulthood, struggling with negative emotions or conflict because they've become so used to deflecting it.

CARETAKER/ENABLER

The caretaker is someone who intuitively takes on responsibility. They feel it's down to them to sort out the family, not realising that, by taking responsibility for others, they can be rescuing people from facing the consequences of their own poor choices and bad behaviour. Often well-intentioned, the caretaker can create more harm when family members are not able to learn from the mistakes they make. When associated with addiction, the enabler can make excuses for the addict, 'clean up' after them and minimise any problems, thereby perpetuating the problem.

DOER

This is the family member who prefers action over all else. They may be very organised, do lots of cooking and household chores, organise the family and generally always be busy doing something. Sometimes this can involve parentification, where a child takes on the responsibilities of a parent/care-giver. As an adult, the doer is always on the go and doesn't know how to slow down and do less. Even though they like doing things, they can become very bitter and resentful when they're not appreciated, while still struggling to say no when anything is asked of them.

MARTYR

Similar to the doer, the martyr 'does so much' for the family. This role is all about sacrificing for the family. They are prone to guilt-tripping, feeling hard done by and generally neglecting themselves. As an adult, this can be a pervasive role that continues, where taking responsibility for others is easier than taking responsibility for themselves and their whole identity becomes about other people and how much they have sacrificed for them.

Family relationships

Below are some questions to help you to explore the child-hood issues relevant to you. Be sure to be as honest with yourself as you can and to include as much detail as possible.

- Describe your relationship with your caregivers when you were little and growing up.
- What do you remember about their relationship with each other?
- How did they speak about and treat each other?
- Was the atmosphere secure, anxious or avoidant?
- Did they have addiction or any mental health issues?
- What kind of a relationship did you have with your siblings?

- How did you feel in those relationships? (For example, safe/supported/scared/teased/bullied/ignored.)
- What is your best memory of when you were little?
- What is your worst memory? Did you have any experiences of inappropriate, unhealthy or abusive behaviour?
- What does each of these memories tell you?
- Did you feel you had to 'do' or 'be' a certain way in order to be acceptable/loved/approved of?
- What did you learn about life and relationships when you were little?

Marco and Jason were like countless other couples I have seen. Marco had a European upbringing and wanted sex and closeness, which seemed impossibly incompatible with Jason's British upbringing, which included little affection and so much neglect he was making his own school lunch from the age of six. The couple not only had a sexless relationship but the atmosphere between them had become hostile and critical. This had been the status quo for several years, so by the time they came to see me, neither could conceal their bitterness. Both felt blamed or resented by the other, and took every opportunity to put the other down.

Taking a deeper look, it emerged that Marco's parents had struggled in their marriage and he could remember overhearing many fights where his father berated his mother for withholding sex and being 'cold'. So too with Jason: his parents had divorced when he was three. His perfectionistic mother felt impossible to please, and was an unfortunate mix of suffocating and emotionally neglecting of Jason all at once.

These childhood experiences had set out the inevitable trajectory for them: they chose people who would
be familiar to them and also fulfil what they had learnt
happened in relationships. They spent much of their
time in therapy (and outside of it too) stuck in blame,
where they both viewed the other person as 'the problem' and themselves the long-suffering victim. It was
very evident they each were stuck in the familiar emotional space of their childhoods: wanting love and
attention, but their loved one being either absent and
withholding, or critical and overbearing.

School experiences

And what about your education and schooling? So much
of our social learning takes place within school and our
friendship groups. We again are confronted with concepts
such as belonging, being accepted, being supported and
safety. In our tough modern world, these can be incredibly painful years. Not only is our intellectual and academic
development under scrutiny, in an environment where it is
possible to fail, but these are often also the years of our
first sexual experiences, huge surges in hormones, forming our identity and a very steep learning curve when it
comes to social engagement. There are so many ways to
feel lost and adrift, overwhelmed and uncertain, and very
alone.

We are painfully aware of the judgement of others in this
stage and it is often the breeding ground for more insecurities, which can further reinforce the belief of how either
kind and compassionate or downright cruel other people
can be.

Consider the questions below. Remember to be as honest with yourself as you can, and to include as much detail as possible.

- How was your school experience? Did you fit in?
- How did you cope with difficult times? (Go to family or teachers/shut down/abuse alcohol or drugs/ behave inappropriately or in self-compromising ways?)
- Did you have crushes?
- Were these your first experiences of yearning (which you recognise in adulthood too)?
- Who were your friends at school and growing up?
- Describe these relationships.
- Did you feel you had to 'do' or 'be' a certain way in order to be acceptable/loved/approved of?
- Did you fit in and feel accepted for who you were?
- Were you able to freely explore and express your sexual orientation and gender identity?
- Did you experience bullying, abuse or trauma?

Romantic Experiences and Past Relationships

Romance and our love lives involve more intense encounters and teach us very comprehensively what we can expect from other people in terms of love, care and tenderness. From crushes to flings, to losing our virginity and into serious partnerships, our romantic history will consolidate so much of our learning, either adding new information – helpful or unhelpful – or further entrenching the lessons already learnt.

The questions opposite are focused on your intimate, romantic and sexual history. However, I suggest you also keep in mind your relationships with certain friends, colleagues and siblings. Our patterns are often very evident in these relationships too. Go through these points for each of your romantic relationships and other key relationships:

Name:

- How did you meet?
- How did you get together?
- What are/were the best aspects of the relationship?
- What are/were the difficulties or struggles for you or the other person?
- What messages do/did you receive from the other person?
- How do you think the relationship is/was for the other person?
- Can you recognise any similar feelings, themes or experiences from your childhood or schooling in this relationship?
- Does/did the other person or what you experienced with the other person remind you of your parents/ caregivers and your experience of them/things that happened when you were young? (For example, infidelity/rejection/being unavailable/being critical/ withholding/being affectionate/being suffocating/ being unpredictable.)
- What are you noticing about the people you choose or let choose you? What is familiar to you about these people and how you feel when you're with them?
- If the relationship ended, how did things end?
- How was the break-up for you? How did you cope?
- How did this relationship affect you? Did it impact your view of relationships?
- How might this have added to or deepened your programming?

Answering these questions will give you a more specific understanding of how your attachment style was formed and how history can repeat itself.

Understanding the Trauma Response and How Our Brains Work

For those of us with insecure ways of relating, a key part of this insecurity is due to some form of attachment trauma. This could be wounding that was great or small, covert or overt, severe or subtle. These experiences are especially powerful if we are infants, children and/or adolescents when they take place, as our developing brains and systems are highly susceptible to disturbances or intrusions, and these formative years are what condition us for what is to come in our future.

Trauma in our attachments when we are growing up is characterised as anything negative that happened to us: inconsistencies and unpredictabilities, as well as all the various forms and degrees of neglect and abuse. Misattunements would also have been hugely influential, whereby our caregivers were not able to attune to our particular needs, as their temperament, personality and reference points were so different (or even opposing) to ours. Indeed, our trauma is not only the negative experiences we may have suffered but also the positive things that we did *not* experience. Often attachment trauma is about a lack – the lack of affection (being held as a child is so vital: it's what soothes the nervous system the most), emotional validation, compassion, understanding and, of course, safety. It can also be brought about by being raised by people with trauma themselves. Whatever its intensity, due to recent breakthroughs in neuroscience, we know that trauma impacts the brain in very specific ways.

Having explored your history above, you will know the various difficulties and traumas that are part of your story and history. The chapters that follow will guide you through how to calm these disturbed and fearful aspects of how you relate.

Ultimately, secure attachment is about being in a healthy, caring relationship, which is only possible with a deactivated nervous system. This allows us to feel safe, calm and secure. We are able to be loving and nurturing, respond supportively to our partners, ask for help when we need it, and sort out conflicts with relative ease.

Anxious and avoidant attachment is maintained by going in and out of trauma response and having an activated nervous system. Because of our insecure attachment, we are constantly triggered into anxiety or avoidance due to the pain and complexity we've experienced because of attachment trauma.

When experiencing difficulty, the trauma responses of fight, flight, freeze or fawn can come into play and put us in survival mode, which isn't helpful in our intimate partnerships. Operating in trauma response can become the status quo and become normalised. Often by the time people come to therapy, they are in a constant state of battling each other. Their nervous systems are activated and they are in survival mode, in equal measure terrified and furious. We all know people in relationships like this. People who argue and complain all the time, who feel nothing about putting each other down in public, who seem to have little warmth between them. This is very much what we want to avoid. Relationships can be our safe place or they can be a war zone. One helps us to heal, grow and feel secure; the other perpetuates our worst fears and keeps us dysregulated, insecure and retraumatising ourselves and each other.

We are so vulnerable in our relationships; our knee-jerk reactivity and defensiveness is a way of managing our vulnerability instinctively. Science teaches us we are built more for war than for love. As adults, our survival depends on us protecting ourselves, not on being loving and kind. On a primal level, we have much more developed instincts for defending ourselves (to the end if necessary), which is evident in our lack of sophisticated relating skills and instead the ease with which we can be combative, argumentative and plain vicious to those we claim to love the most.

When negative and unhealthy ways of relating have become the norm in our relationships, we need to pay attention. We are not doing right by ourselves or the other person. We must think deeply about changing what we are doing and healing our trauma responses as we do not want this misery to be entrenched.

Our work, if we want our experience of love to improve, is to resist our warring tendencies and develop in ourselves the capacity and willingness to put down our attachment defences and to transform our partners from enemies into wonderful friends and trusted lovers.

When we are in survival mode – in fight, flight, freeze or fawn – this isn't a cuddly, tender space. We believe we are fighting for our lives and when that is the case, empathy is not needed. On the contrary, we often need rage and contempt to fuel our need to fight. Compassion goes out the window and we are self-centred in the extreme. If we were fighting for our life, this would be appropriate. However, in our romantic relationships, we need to work hard to make a secure base for ourselves and our partners. Safety comes when there is not a threat of imminent danger or fighting. When we can be accepted and loved. When the people in the relationship strive to be compassionate and caring to one another.

Learning how to regulate our nervous system – through understanding our patterns and scripts, breathing and emotional regulation techniques (which we'll explore in Part III) – is the best thing we can do to help us in our relationships. Once we are in control of our nervous systems, we are in control of how we relate and love.

The Story of Our Lives

We're all living a specific version of our lives, known as our script, and in our insecure attachment it will be negative and self-defeating. Our script is the lens through which we view ourselves and the world. Based on our past, personality, environment, experiences and relationships, our brains form narratives to make sense of what has happened in our lives. Often our script can be negative in nature and is at the root of our distress. By following this script, we recreate the same relational experiences and responses over and over again – we think the same thoughts and act out the same behaviour, which will lead to the same outcomes. This reinforces the negativity and unhealthy beliefs they encapsulate. Examples of typical scripts in relationships include:

> 'Relationships never work out for me.'
> 'I'm always the one doing all the emotional work in relationships.'
> 'No one understands me.'
> 'I am not enough.'
> 'My life is so stressful – it's one thing after another.'
> 'I never fit in anywhere I go.'
> 'People always let me down.'

By recognising our unconscious scripts, we can start to do things differently, and that is how we can help ourselves grow and get more of what we want.

Making the Unconscious Conscious

If we are not aware of why we are reacting the way we are, why we view things the way we do, why we interpret things how we do and why we choose what we choose, we are not in charge of our own lives. We are unconsciously perpetuating the patterns that have been programmed in us long ago. We will not make decisions based on our health, our well-being or what is best for us; we will make decisions based on our stories and our belief systems. Unless we increase our awareness, making the unconscious more conscious, we will continue to take ourselves down well-worn roads that do not lead to where we want to go.

Our unconscious fears can often be working in direct opposition to what we hope and wish for.

Our unhelpful script embodies all the unmet needs and traumas of early childhood, which are repeatedly reinforced and re-enacted in adult life in our intimate relationships. It influences how we relate to ourselves and others. This book is about making these hugely powerful unconscious processes more conscious so we can rewrite our scripts and break our patterns. This is so we can take control of what our future will be like, rather than unconsciously recreating 'the story of our lives'.

Any kind of personal development work is first and foremost about raising our awareness. It's about doing the very difficult work of bringing conscious focus to our highly unconscious actions and mindsets. If we don't know that we are actually very fearful of intimacy and close connections, for example, we will never be able to work on that. We will believe our conscious thought that we want relationships and be confused and hurt when we can't sustain one, not knowing that unconsciously we might be pushing people away or sabotaging our partnerships to *make sure* we don't get too close to anyone.

It's therefore so important to identify the specific patterns and narratives we live by that need to be changed if we are to love differently. With this in mind, write down which of the following themes are familiar to you:

- not feeling heard
- not feeling important
- feeling dismissed or patronised
- feeling your feelings don't matter
- feeling disrespected
- feeling criticised
- feeling smothered
- feeling taken for granted
- feeling fine but your partner isn't happy
- feeling insecure
- add your own: _____

These are your tender spots.

You will have sensitivity around these feelings, and whenever you feel them you will likely become reactive (get triggered) and your scripts will come out. Becoming conscious of these wounded parts of you is important as they will help you understand when one of your patterns might be playing out. It's imperative you recognise when you've been triggered, as getting triggered all the time is part of maintaining your patterns.

What's your script?

Upon reflection, our scripts can be very obvious – they could be statements we say all the time or even mantras we live by. Or they can be hidden deep in our unconscious but revealed by our beliefs and insecurities. Read through the examples below and see which strike a chord. Consider not only what resonates but also what might help make sense of some of your history or relational experiences.

Some typical life stories and themes:

- I never get what I want.
- I am not enough.
- People always leave me.
- I don't matter to anyone.
- What I want doesn't matter.
- I don't deserve love.
- Whatever I do it's never enough.
- Life is endlessly difficult. It's one negative thing after another.
- Hell is other people.
- I can't trust other people.
- Things don't work out for me.
- Other people try to trap me.
- It's always my fault.
- If people knew the real me, they wouldn't like me.
- I'm no good at relationships.
- I have to do everything.
- It's better to be alone.
- No one understands me.
- Add your own: _____

Anxiously attached individuals might recognise scripts around not getting the love you want and people being disappointing. **Avoidantly attached individuals** might recognise scripts around not being understood or preferring to be on your own. Regardless, these scripts paint a sad – and inaccurate – picture of what is possible from love and relationships. Yes, they may come from experiences you have had; however, those are specific instances in your life. Our scripts magnify them into blanket statements where no other options are possible. These are entirely based on our fears and can act as very powerful barriers to getting close to others.

By first uncovering our scripts and then learning ways to challenge and change these themes (which we'll do in Part II), we will not be doomed to repeat our mistakes or our hurts.

We all have scripts but very few of us are aware of them or the extent to which they dominate our lives. Having conscious understanding of why we do what we do, and recognising when we are playing out our scripts and patterns, liberates us to start doing things differently, to take responsibility for our choices and behaviour, and to write our own next chapter.

Journalling prompts

- Can you recognise that you had some unhelpful or difficult experiences growing up and throughout your life which may have impacted how much you trust, respect or believe you can rely on people today? What were they?
- Are you aware of trauma responses and the ways in which they play out for you in your relationships? Describe.
- What key behaviours of yours would you like to change, both in your relationships and within yourself? What specific fears are holding you back?
- Which scripts in your life do you most wish to change?
- Write down how you might experience relationships differently if you were not playing out these patterns.

PART II

Identifying Your Relationship Patterns

With our attachment styles come some very identifiable patterns of relating that can be predictable, or they can be unique to some very specific circumstances of our lives. Generally, though, they will have themes that pertain to our attachment wounds.

In this section, I have outlined a few possible patterns that could play out in your relational life. This is by no means an exhaustive list, but rather food for thought to help you to consider what patterns might be at play for you and how they manifest in your life and relationships. Patterns are on a continuum, so can range from mild to moderate to extreme. Make a note of the ones that resonate with you, their extremity, and also add your own. Again, you may select tendencies from all the different attachment styles. Think of specific relationships as you consider these.

CHAPTER 3

Anxious Attachment Traits and Tendencies

When our anxious attachment is triggered, our thoughts and feelings *feel so real*. We treat our concerns as facts, and react to life and relationships as if all the bad stuff we fear is actually happening. Anxious attachment is like any anxiety: in extremes, we catastrophise, we have intrusive thoughts, we feel tense and restless, we have a sense of impending danger or panic, our hearts race and we want to control whatever it is that is 'causing' the anxiety. We have trouble sleeping, have gastrointestinal problems, worry, are hypervigilant, people-please, try to be perfect, proximity-seek, want reassurance, complain, over-function and *expect* to be hurt and rejected. It is hell on earth.

We can lose control of our emotions, and they control us because everything feels so real and alarming. Our nervous system is reacting to what we believe are genuine dangers (see page 65). In attachment terms, when we are anxiously attached, the full force of our fear makes us hold on tight to our partners, as safety means being close, and distance or separation from our partners is a significant threat.

Lucy had been with her partner for 18 months and they had just moved in together. She knew she was very important to him but struggled with out-of-control emotion when she was left alone at home. When this happened, she wanted contact, lots of contact, from her partner and, sometimes, when Lucy couldn't get hold of him, she would panic and message him repeatedly. Then she would call repeatedly. She would go on his social media, send messages, comment and, finally, threaten. Her fear of rejection and abandonment was so great she descended into fearful, desperate proximity-seeking. Having been neglected a lot in her younger years, being home alone brought back too many unconscious associations. She hated herself for her behaviour and knew her partner hated it too. When exploring it with her, we discovered if she didn't hear from him or know he was 'there', she felt like she might die. This was a very young trauma she was re-experiencing agonisingly in the here and now.

It's extremely important to recognise the unhelpful and sometimes traumatised thinking and feeling we have in our anxiously attached state.

Feeling so much is extremely painful, and it is especially painful when we are met with a lack of feeling in our partners. It is often the lacklustre emotional responsiveness of the other person that is the most triggering and exacerbating of the feelings which can create so much of our suffering. When our anxiety is activated our view of relationships is skewed to the negative. We feel so much. Too much.

Often, we are carrying the emotions for the relationship,

as we are the ones who are the most sensitive and emotionally aware. So we absorb all the emotions in the environment, we take them on and unconsciously add them to our labour. This is a heavy load to carry. As the feelers in the relationship, we can become overwhelmed by all the emotion we are left to digest and make sense of.

Having emotions is a positive thing – we are fortunate to have the capacity to have a human, emotional experience. However, it also means we can be impulsive and lose rational perspective; we can jump to the worst-case scenario, negatively interpret our partners' behaviour or comments, and escalate discussions into conflict. We can become hugely preoccupied about our partners – how they feel about us, their presence in our lives, how much they care, how they need to change, how things need to get better and how wrong everything is.

At the same time all of this is happening, we can be torn. We want attention and validation, but we are ambivalent too. The research shows that, when anxiously attached, we experience painful and conflicting emotions whereby we desperately want the reassuring presence of our partners, but, at the same time, we feel confusion and anger having them in our lives, and want to punish or push them away. We've learnt that other people are unreliable when it comes to caring for us, and we're furious. We want closeness but we also are worried the people we're with don't want to be with us. Like I said, it can be hell.

What we feel when our anxious attachment has been activated

These are some of the behavioural and emotional experiences that can occur when we are in a state of anxious attachment:

- Upset and preoccupied with what we're not getting in our relationship.
- Pervasive dissatisfaction with the relationship.
- Highly motivated (and anxious) to work on the relationship and 'make things better'.
- Cycling between happiness, anger, frustration, sadness, confusion and numbness.
- Fear of being rejected or abandoned.
- Fury when we're not getting what we want, or when feeling hurt or misunderstood.
- Panic when our partners are moving away.
- Bitter and resentful as we begin to feel burnt out in the relationship.
- Overwhelmed by our partners' problems or our own lack of happiness in the relationship.
- Hurt and wanting to punish our partners in various ways.
- Exhausted and at the end of our tether.
- Giving up and feeling devastated or fatigued as an ambivalent phase sets in.

These are some of the coping strategies we may use when in a state of anxious attachment:

- reassurance-seeking
- proximity-seeking
- needing others to regulate us
- idealising our partners
- hating ourselves
- being hypervigilant to any temperature changes in our relationships and partners
- being overly accommodating

- rarely saying no
- being hostile
- always 'working' on the relationship
- trying to control our partners
- over-focusing on others
- getting angry and pushing people away when finally fed up
- overthinking everything
- catastrophising as a way of protecting ourselves from 'inevitable' disappointment

Anxious Traits

Let's look at our anxious ways of relating that require our attention. These are the behaviours and thinking patterns that reinforce our insecurity and prevent safety in our relationships with others and peace within ourselves. The chapters in Part III will give you the tools to shift away from these defensive ways of being to more secure ways of relating. You may recognise all of these or simply a few.

Low self-esteem and bad choices in partners

It is a sad truth that due to the lack of consistency and care we experienced in our childhood relationships, we will be drawn and attracted to people in adult relationships who can also neglect us. There's a high probability we will unconsciously choose people who are not going to be in keeping with what we want and deserve and, because of the reinforcing nature of our decision-making, we can be in a perpetual cycle of making bad choices in partners.

We will all have our type. When asked, people will say things like 'tall, dark and handsome, funny with a cheeky smile', but what may be much more accurate could be 'dark features, drinks too much, can be charming initially but then is emotionally closed off and can't communicate'. And *that* will likely be very familiar to us.

Our type is much less about physical features (although those can definitely be a thing too) than it is about the relational experience we have with intimate partners – how it *feels* when we're with them and what takes place within the relationship. Generally, their level of interest, availability, consideration, maturity and attachment style will have clear echoes from our past if we take the time to reflect on them. So too will the themes that play out within our relationships, like addictions, attitudes to money, controlling behaviour, anxiety or depression, anger, being the victim or martyr, infidelity or legal issues, to name a few. It's shocking how history keeps repeating itself. Sometimes it's literally copy and paste.

It's unrealistic for us to expect ourselves to simply go for completely different people. I think it is okay and inevitable to have a type; however, I encourage you to pay attention to how extreme the person you are interested in is. If someone is completely unreachable and unavailable, not interested on working on themselves or loving you, being considerate or growing, there is very little for you to work with. The fact that history does keep repeating itself shows us how important it is for our partners to be on board with changing our default trajectories.

The winning combination is when everyone in a relationship is prepared to grow. You may not be growing at the same rate or in the same ways, but as long as someone is not completely fixed and rigid in their position, with no interest in changing, a new kind of relationship can be created – with a new future to go with it.

Signs your partner isn't willing to grow

- Mistakes their unhelpful traits and behaviours (like anger or problem drinking) for 'who they are'.
- Blames you for all the relationship's problems.
- Doesn't think anything is wrong with them.
- Thinks therapy and personal growth is navel-gazing and indulgent.
- Is fixed in the defensive position when discussing issues.
- Can't take criticism or feedback (has an answer for everything).
- Thinks attending/sitting in a chair in therapy is 'doing the work'/'doing everything they can'.
- Says, 'I don't think I need to change.'

Anticipating rejection

Is there anything more likely to keep our nervous system activated than imagining we are about to be rejected at any moment? Abandonment is one of our core fears and in our anxiously attached state we are always braced for rejection. We can read it in many situations, interpreting our partners' tone of voice or focus elsewhere as an imminent danger. This increases our hypervigilance, where we notice every temperature change, or real or perceived mood shift in our partners and our environment. We are primed, ready and waiting for the inevitable pain. This is exhausting and will absolutely sabotage our ability to be secure and confident in our relationships.

A part of abandonment fear is a terror of being alone. When we are anxiously attached, in extremis, our fear of being alone is tantamount to a fear of dying. That's because this fear will come from a childhood when being left on our own was life-threatening. So, when our attachment trauma has been triggered, we are not thinking as competent adults, we are looking through the lens of our trauma, because, at one point, being left represented a threat to our survival. The fear of being alone is much more far-reaching than we sometimes realise.

Emotional caretaking and over-functioning

Do you have the weight of the world on your shoulders? Do you take responsibility for everything that needs to be worked on in the relationship? Are you the feeler in a relationship, full of emotion and sometimes overwhelm, while your partner is cut off and shut-down? When we become the emotional caretakers in our partnerships, we can over-function, doing all or too much of the emotional labour of partnership, overworking ourselves and compromising ourselves in the process. We relieve people of their own responsibility by doing their share, and we can become resentful and angry because there are such imbalances.

There's a difference between being caring and being a caretaker. Being caring is crucial to our relationships and is not something we ever want to change. However, we can cross the line into caretaking very easily. Caretaking is when we have lost control and we are no longer choosing our behaviour, rather doing everything from a place of 'should' or 'need to'. We don't say no. We don't look after ourselves and we are at risk of burn-out. It's people-pleasing on steroids. We can get anxious or depressed as the emotional load becomes too much.

Underneath our over-functioning is a deep desire to be loved and accepted. We maybe received little validation growing up and, when we did, it was because of something we *did*. We learnt that doing is the best way of getting attention from the people most important to us. We also learnt that if we did things for other people we could be needed, which wasn't as good as being loved but we would settle for it anyway. A need to be needed is simply a need to be loved that has adapted to the environment.

We must do the difficult work of doing less, getting used to sitting on our hands more and letting others do their rightful share (there are tips to help you with this in Chapter 10). We avoid doing this because we may not like to see how other people turn up for us (or not) in our relationships, which is why it's doubly important we take the time to notice.

Examples of caretaking

- Doing something for someone they could do for themselves.
- Giving unsolicited advice/always trying to be 'helpful'.
- Believing you know what's best for someone and being dominating as a result.
- Over-focusing on someone else (often while neglecting yourself).
- Being over-involved in other people's lives.
- Taking responsibility for things that aren't your responsibility.
- Trying to control people and outcomes.
- Thinking that worrying and complaining are part of caring for someone.
- Overworking and being overly emotionally invested.
- Feeling angry and annoyed when people don't do what you want them to do.
- Thinking obsessively about someone else and their problems.
- Not having boundaries with others when it comes to your time, energy or money.

Chronic dissatisfaction and setting your partner up to fail

We might think we are desperate to be satisfied in relationships, that we want nothing more than peace and happiness, but we can have a powerful unconscious process at play. As discussed before, insecure attachment is self-perpetuating. Anxious attachment is about *maintaining* our anxiety. We are always looking for things to be anxious about and that is why we experience chronic dissatisfaction – we will unconsciously reject any positives, minimise loving acts, dismiss reassurances, downplay the good, or actively demonise our partners and all that they do. It's possible we do not know how to be satisfied; we only know how to be dissatisfied and believe we always will be.

Part of this is caused by having an unconscious investment in our partners' failing (in our eyes) and wanting to stay in the victim position. This is evident when our partners feel they cannot win with us, nothing is ever good enough and they are hurt and exhausted (and have often given up). This is us pushing our partners away. It's a way of controlling an outcome we feel is inevitable – being disappointed – so we simply start to live in a disappointed state all the time. Sometimes we are let down before our partners have even done anything.

In setting up our partners to fail, we will unconsciously create numerous scenarios and situations on a regular basis in which they are unlikely or unable to please us, so all our fears and insecurities will be confirmed.

We ourselves are rejecting and unkind, shut down, withhold affection and sex, shake our heads and roll our eyes – and then feel deeply wounded because we feel so lonely and unloved.

Do you set up your partner to fail?

- Unconsciously pushing their buttons and then blaming them for being reactive.
- Sabotaging or criticising their efforts.
- Expecting them to rescue you.
- Excluding them from important discussions.
- Projecting your bad mood on to them.
- Not giving them a chance to help.
- Expecting them to mess up and then highlighting their inadequacy if they do.
- Making unrealistic demands on their time.
- Playing to their weaknesses rather than their strengths.

What is cognitive bias?

Our brains make very quick judgements and are influenced by our conscious and unconscious emotions, prejudices, assumptions and associations. Due to the subjective nature of our perspectives, we can come to conclusions based on false or inaccurate data, as interpreted by our limited understanding and experience.

The halo effect (positive bias) is when we see a person as wholly good, having only seen one positive feature or trait, not taking time to get to know them better or understand the full picture.

The horn effect (negative bias) is when we categorise someone or something as wholly negative, having seen a single negative aspect (or a couple). We don't value or take into account anything that might deviate from our negative view of them.

What's very important to understand about bias is how unconscious and fixed it is. Once we've made a decision or formed an opinion, we will unconsciously look for information that *confirms* our opinion, often discrediting and ignoring any information that doesn't – this is known as **confirmation bias**. In our intimate partnerships, this is reductive and prevents us from truly knowing our partners or understanding our relationships.

Mental preoccupation

We have grown accustomed to being preoccupied with our relationships in such a detailed way it can be unhealthy. In doing so, we can inadvertently become fault-finders and complainers – things that both fuel anxious attachment *and* push our partners away. This is what perpetuates the pattern.

The preoccupation aspect of anxious attachment is one of our most deeply entrenched behaviours and sometimes we can be so focused on our relationships that our careers, friendships, creativity and life in general can be neglected.

Signs that you are hyper-focused on your relationship

- Your relationship dominates your headspace.
- You can become overly critical.

- You are hypervigilant and can pick up on your partner's mood, language or micro expressions.
- You constantly talk about your relationship to friends and family.
- You overthink and catastrophise what's happening in your relationship.
- You panic when you perceive their attention is not on you.
- You can be deeply wounded if they seem not to want to spend time with you.

We have learnt to be tuned into what is going on for the people around us. We've learnt to notice people's reactions and responses. We've learnt to notice people's moods. We are astute and intuitive. And we are very concerned with what people might be thinking about us. We can be heavily influenced by people's thoughts and opinions, and we find it very difficult if we imagine people are thinking or feeling negatively about us.

Not being liked or approved of felt dangerous when we were younger, and in adulthood now, we continue to give other people that power.

Feeling discomfort in silence, space and separateness

When our anxious attachment is activated, part of our belief system dictates that we need to keep our partners extremely close because if they are not we mistakenly believe our relationship is in jeopardy. We assume the person's feelings for us are not as strong as they should be. In our desire for closeness, we can misinterpret natural and healthy space and separateness in relationships as rejecting and hurtful. This can increase our anxiety and the unhealthy behaviours that go with it.

To help ourselves, we can recognise that the proximity and intensity we like in relationships is not always possible. Acknowledging that silence, space and separateness often happen in loving adult partnerships, and are neither unusual nor dangerous, can help us tolerate the discomfort when they occur.

Secure relationships consist of individuals independently going about their lives and sharing those lives with each other. In our proximity-seeking, we can try to merge our lives, emotionally and physically, with our partners', and this is not healthy. We need to breathe into this discomfort so we can learn to tolerate and eventually desensitise to appropriate (and secure) space. Breathwork exercises are covered in Chapter 7.

Excessive reassurance-seeking

It is normal to sometimes want reassurance from our partners. This offers a moment of vulnerability and intimacy and can make a relationship stronger. Seeking reassurance is ideally a trust-building exercise. However, if we require huge amounts of reassurance and that reassurance does not build trust and closeness in the partnership, it may well be an anxious process and therefore could be part of the problem rather than the solution.

When we are constantly seeking reassurance, it often means we are not receiving or taking in that assurance when we receive it. A need for excessive reassurance could manifest in behaviours like wanting to be told you are loved countless times a day, liking to receive multiple messages when your partner is out without you, or becoming panicky if your partner doesn't hold your hand, or hug or kiss you, or want to have sex all the time.

Our partners may communicate incredibly loving and supportive statements that embody their care and generosity of spirit. They might share movingly about how important we are to them and how much we are loved. And yet our anxious attachment discards it all. Reassurance is all around us but anxious attachment can make it invisible. We must learn to let in reassurance and to notice it in the many ways it is expressed. I also suggest noticing and allowing in other reassuring factors that we often dismiss or miss:

- If someone chooses to have us in their life and continues to choose us every day, that is concrete confirmation of their desire to be with us.
- When someone performs acts of service, like sorting out admin, doing practical things or making a meal.
- When someone looks at us and smiles fondly.
- When someone puts in effort with our friends and family.
- When someone is a loyal presence in our life, reliable and steadfast.

At the mercy of our negative emotions

One of the most painful experiences we have when we are anxiously attached is losing control of our feelings and, in turn, losing control of our behaviour. This can lead to us doing and saying things about which we can later feel very upset, ashamed or regretful. We can lose our cool and berate our partners, or we can be so frightened that we plead with our partners in not-very-esteeming ways. In fact, we will do whatever we can in order to get our partners to reduce our anxiety. We will sweet-talk, demand, beg, cajole, seduce, criticise, charm, insult, force, cry, manipulate or threaten.

When we are triggered or deeply upset our emotional experience is so profoundly convincing that it is very difficult for us to recognise we are being controlled by our feelings and can be operating in extreme and unhelpful ways. As part of anxious attachment, we are hyperfocused on the problem and that's going to quickly become a distorted view where only negatives exist.

Whereas avoidance is a shutting down process, anxious attachment is a doing process. Sometimes there is internal doing – like fretting, ruminating, catastrophising and projecting – and sometimes it is external – like overexplaining, micromanaging and generally doing and saying too much. When we are behaving in this way, anxious attachment is in the driving seat.

Learning to tolerate anxious feelings when we experience them can allow us to take charge of what we are doing more often. This will be explored in Chapter 7.

Trust issues

The vast majority of our anxious behaviour reveals how little trust we have. The hypervigilance and hyperfunctioning, the preoccupation and the controlling behaviour, all speak of us not trusting other people to do right by us. We believe that, unless we're there, making it happen, chances are we will be forgotten or neglected. We need to be policing and managing, monitoring and checking, shepherding and patrolling; this is the sad legacy of what we learnt growing up or from previous relationships. We are accustomed to people not meeting our needs. Learning to trust others can be extremely hard for us because people are not going to do what we want. They may not do what we want in the timeframe we want it, and they most certainly won't do what we want in the manner we want it done.

Having trust issues after hurt, pain and betrayal is natural and appropriate, but we must be careful not to get stuck there. Being defensive does not protect us. It keeps people away from us, exacerbates loneliness, and reinforces the idea that other people don't care about us. Appropriate risk-taking is part of putting ourselves out there for relationships.

Perhaps our hearts have hardened or we have become bitter and cynical. The truth is, we don't let people in. That is the work of learning to trust: letting people be part of our lives, letting people share our world.

Trust isn't all or nothing, it's earned – bit by bit. Tolerating vulnerability and taking micro-risks can help us to create healthy relationships and bring us peace.

It is trusting the world and others to not be actively *against us* as we go about our lives.

How to work on your trust issues

There are many reasons for trust issues and it's certainly not unhealthy to be cautious and protect ourselves. However, if our trust issues are keeping us from having relaxed, fulfilling relationships and impacting our self-esteem and mental and emotional well-being, it's something for us to work on.

Here are some signs of trust issues:

- You are bitter and cynical, jaded and closed off.
- You expect to be hurt.
- You are easily angered and overly protective or defensive.

- You keep others at an emotional arm's length.
- You are scared of real commitment and intimacy.
- You fault-find and don't forgive the smallest mistakes.
- You are excessively wary of people.
- You feel lonely and alone.

It's important to recognise the meaning of trust. Some things that may help you to let go of issues with trust include:

1. Accept we are all flawed and imperfect - we will make mistakes and let people down. We can try to accept this as part of being human.
2. Understand trust doesn't have to be given out freely. It's okay to wait for people to earn it before deciding we can rely on them. We can work on being receptive and staying cautiously optimistic.
3. Take emotional risks. Practise bravery and allow yourself to be vulnerable. Take micro-risks to develop trust slowly over time.
4. Explore why you're scared and what you're scared of so you can process those experiences, heal what you can, and attempt to move on into a better future.
5. Trust again. And again. If you fail and revert back to mistrusting tendencies, have compassion for yourself. Trust again. Keep putting yourself out there, don't become bitter. You deserve love and care.

Struggling to understand adult love versus childhood love

I wonder how many of us were 'Daddy's Little Stars' or 'Mother's Little Helpers'? Often these were aspects of our first heady love affair we had with our parents/caregivers growing up. Maybe they rewarded us for being cute, helpful or achieving, and we experienced magical moments with them as a result. An intensity of love is therefore imprinted in our nervous and attachment systems, and, because these extraordinary moments were so irresistible and delicious, but were just moments or scarce, we can chase that feeling for the rest of our lives.

This goes some way to explaining why we are chronically dissatisfied in our relationships and why people fall short of our unconscious, fantastical expectations. We had a brief taste of the ecstasy of 'special' relationships early on and have been aching for it ever since. Nothing is likely to ever come close, certainly not in the long term. That might also be why we are drawn to particularly intense people and relationships, and can have dramatic, dysfunctional relationships as a way of manifesting that high, and also experience those strangely compelling lows.

Part of becoming secure is letting go of the magical thinking idea of what adult love might be like. The relationships, or moments, we shared with our parents/caregivers growing up are very specific to the parent–child relationship. As we emotionally mature, we can realise that adult relationships are different in tone and feeling.

Some of us have a secret desire to be rescued, while others want the total adoration of an enthralled parent/caregiver, and we need to realise that that is not healthy or realistic in our present lives. We can learn the difference between a child's love and an adult lover. Many of us, however, think they are the same.

Feeling anxious and resentful most of the time

When our anxious attachment is activated, how we experience life can be very distressing indeed. We can become angry people in the world and our relationships, or we can be forever worrying and fretting about something. Sometimes our anxiety and resentment are purely defensive, and we are stuck in some kind of fight response, where it's us against the world.

When we are hyperfunctioning and doing too much, we're not taking good care of ourselves and we are wanting more from people, despite not being able to ask for help or say no when we are overworked. So we get resentful. We stew. We feel taken for granted, underappreciated, neglected and victimised. These reactions were often modelled to us by one of our parents/caregivers and we learnt the lesson very well.

We can become bags of nerves or unpleasant to be around. We can be irritable and snippy, or impossible to please and controlling. This is the emotional territory of anxious attachment, as well as many other things that we can suffer from: trauma, depression, perfectionism, chronic illness, people-pleasing, burn-out, stress-related illness, insomnia, eating disorders, work compulsion or drug and alcohol dependence. Bringing compassion to ourselves is vital and is covered in part III.

When ending a relationship, we experience it as a death

Relationships end all the time. It's part of life, certainly a part of our modern lives. But for those of us with anxious attachment, if our relationship ends badly, we can feel seismic emotions. A relationship ending represents a letting go that is completely at odds with every one of our anxiously attached beliefs; it mainlines straight into our deepest attachment trauma. It can feel like a total wrench, a death, even. How we view relationships was crystallised when we were little, when our survival depended on us being connected to our caregivers. Without those relationships, we would risk death. Our attachment system is frozen in that time. When relationships end, it feels profoundly dangerous on the most primitive level. All our early-life neglect and abandonment collide with the present-day rejection of an ending, and we may respond in all manner of grief, terror, fawning, rage, anxiety and depression. Sometimes this can be very pronounced and overtly experienced. Or it can be quite subtle and covertly experienced – it is more of an implosion, our pain manifesting in ruminations, intrusive thoughts, fantasies, nostalgia and obsessiveness.

Because of this, relationships that don't work out are retraumatising. They reinforce and confirm all our negative beliefs, further entrenching our insecure attachment and all the sorrow it encapsulates.

Uncontained and compulsive venting

When worked up, some of us are not known for our restraint. In fact, we can be the over-explaining, incessantly criticising, resentment-blurting, anger-wielding, passive-aggressive, lesson-teaching, unhappy people who cross lines and boundaries with recklessness and disregard for consequences. While our avoidant counterparts do too little, we do too much. And that goes for our style of communicating too. We can compulsively message or call. We can write paragraphs in messages. We can reel off lists of hurts committed against us. We can work ourselves up and not have boundaries around how much we complain and criticise.

This is at the heart of dysregulation. When we are triggered, we can very easily go into fight response, which will involve us barraging our partners with our hurt, disappointment, rage and fear. We can experience a tidal wave of pain that washes over us and can flood us, our partners and our relationships.

This behaviour can do a lot of damage. We want to be understood and heard, but because we are dysregulated and not in control, we go too far and allow our hurt and pain to come out destructively.

Lack of self-compassion

When we look to others to regulate us and make us feel okay, we often miss out on developing something incredibly important: self-compassion. For so long, we have failed to feel the love that we deserve. Unfortunately, the luxury of feeling sure we are loved is not part of our inner experience. Instead, we've had to sing for our supper, 'earning' approval and care, and we are full of desperation, sadness, fury and despair as a result. But then we can hate ourselves for our behaviour, thereby continuing our pattern of no one being there to tend to us and care for us in our times of need. Sooner or later, we have to be the ones who will step in and, through repeated and loving acts of care, look after ourselves and return us to a place of regulated calm and trust.

Bringing compassion to our view of ourselves is an important step in becoming secure. It's heartbreaking we did not feel sure of love, but instead anxious. It's sad we feel we need to over-function and 'work' in order to earn attention, if not love. We have every right to feel compassion for our young selves and for us today. And by bringing compassion to ourselves, we are then able to soothe ourselves and can begin treating ourselves with some of the tenderness and the care that we needed when we were younger. We can be there for ourselves, with comfort and a kind word. This will help us to deactivate our nervous system and return to a gentler place.

Staying too long in unhealthy relationships

Part of anxious attachment is holding on tight. Our primary aim is not to find someone we are compatible with, who respects us and with whom we could create a wonderful life; rather, our immediate and pressing (unconscious) aim is to make sure we are not rejected. That means whoever we are dating or in a relationship with needs to be someone who chooses us.

Our need for attention, acceptance and validation from others is all-encompassing. We do not come from a secure place where we are evaluating whether someone is right for us; we come from an insecure place of needing to be liked, lusted after and loved. Our focus therefore is purely on making sure we are in a relationship and not being rejected. The quality of the relationship can matter little. Because of this, we can often spend far too long in relationships that are not good or healthy for us. We will soldier on until the bitter end, staying for months or years in a relationship that clearly will not fulfil us.

Just as we fall in love too easily, we stay fighting for relationships long after they have expired. It can be hard for us to walk away from people and relationships because our instinct is to hold on, stay together and do whatever it takes, regardless of pain, happiness or compatibility. When we're terrified of falling the last thing we want to do is let go.

Dependency issues

There's a huge irony at play for us. We can feel so dependent in our relationships, desperately wanting others to take care of us and be there for us. We can feel separate and lost when we are not in a relationship, or when we are in an unhappy relationship. We think we need other people there so we can tackle life. But the truth is we are some of the most competent, capable, high-achieving people out there. We are the people who can get things done, complete the tasks, do the research, perform very well in our jobs, raise families, contribute to communities and who other people come to for advice and support.

Our dependency is an emotional dependency. Out in the world, we can do life with great efficiency. It's when we are in relationships that our dependency issues are triggered, and part of our anxious attachment is feeling so vulnerable and powerless. We need to unlearn these associations, bringing the strong and self-determining parts of ourselves into our partnerships so we can show up robust, and adult, when the vulnerability strikes. Chapters 7 and 10 will show you exactly how to do this.

It's natural to want care from our partners, to want to be loved and cherished, but we can participate in relationships from a place of our own self-sufficiency. We can remove the hyperfocus on our partners and return our efforts to our own lives. We will have goals and dreams of our own, and these need to be our priority. We do not need to be quite so preoccupied with our partners and relationships, instead, lovingly tending to our own lives and all we wish to achieve.

Need for control

Feeling so out of control much of the time, we will attempt to control most things to try to compensate for this. Yet, one of the biggest mistakes we can make is thinking that we can control other people.

We can be precoccupied with other people, the way they need to change, and our enormous efforts to try to change them. It is an unbelievably difficult pill to swallow that we are powerless over other people. As part of our over-responsibility, we often take responsibility for other people's behaviour and feel it is down to us to do something about it.

One of the biggest lessons we have to learn in order to challenge anxious attachment is that the tightest grip is with an open hand. Our grip can tighten very quickly when our anxiety appears. We so desperately want things to go our way, to get the love we crave, to know we matter to others, to make everything okay, to have happy families, to be loved and accepted. These cravings can control us if we're not careful, and it can make us controlling. It's hard for us to leave people to their own devices because we want things from others. We want their attention and validation, and we don't want them to behave in ways that are painful or go against our wishes. We need to keep a healthy perspective and realise we can't do other people's work for them. We'll explore this further in Chapter 10.

Having sex when we want love

What are the reasons you have sex? Some of us have sex in an attempt to be liked by the other person. We may feel that we are not enough to be loved in our own right and instead we need to be doing or giving something. Being sexual is a way of winning people's affection. In our relationships, this means we can view sex in a functional way, having sex when we want to feel loved. Sex can also sometimes leave us feeling empty or used. We might prioritise our partners' pleasure and fake orgasms or be performative in ways we think we should, or we imagine others think we should.

When dating or single, we can engage in one-night stands and casual sex encounters, even when we don't want to, looking for affection and hoping sex might lead to something more serious. Again, this can reinforce our belief in the transactional nature of sex, leading us to further disconnect from the pleasure and care of sex. We then feel further disillusioned about what we are to other people and question 'why' they are with us.

Falling in love before we've really got to know people

Despite all our fear, we can fall in love so easily. And quickly. Before we even know much about someone we are attached – hook, line and sinker. However, it matters who we invite in; it will have a huge impact on our well-being and our future.

By taking our time getting to know someone, we might come up against some unpalatable realities about them. We might be forced to see things we don't want to see. We might have to confront disappointment. These are all things we try to avoid at the beginning. We want to believe the fantasy, we want to believe what we want to believe, and we can ignore some important information that has been clearly shown to us. We need to have our heart *and* our eyes wide open when getting to know people.

We can slow things down at the beginning. It takes time after the initial honeymoon period to see people's true colours. When the infatuation starts to fade, what is the person like? How do they handle stress? How reliable are they? How kind are they to others? Are they loving? All of this takes time to truly discover.

The first few months and years of a relationship are key. They are the foundation for everything. It's when we learn the most about each other and it's also when we are the most willing to adapt and change to earn the love and respect of the object of our affection. So it is a prime time in which to teach one another how to love each other, when both parties are at their most motivated. We can clearly show our partners what it is we want and need from relationships.

What we can do instead is squander this time pretending to be perfect, not having any needs and not noticing any potential problems. This is a true waste.

How to show your partner what you want

- When they ask what you would like to do/eat/ watch, tell them.
- Have discussions about previous relationships/life experiences, and what you learnt that you cherish and what you find difficult.
- After sex, describe the bits you loved the most.
- Be firm about behaviour you don't like – don't try to be 'easy-breezy'.
- When your partner does something good, be effusive and appreciative.
- Request what you would like as much as possible – this teaches your partner what you want, what life with you will be like and how compatible you are.
- Have needs and have standards. Consider what yours are and live by them.

Stuck in the victim position

Our anxiety is about fear. And when we are fearful we do not feel powerful. In fact, often, we feel overpowered and that other people are threatening us or are out to get us. We are in a familiar story where other people are causing us pain and we are victims of their maliciousness, manipulativeness or ignorance. While this is understandable in human interactions, and often we *are* the victim of people's bad behaviour and poor judgements, when our anxious attachment is triggered we can get stuck in victim mentality.

We see ourselves as the slighted, hard-done-by party and operate from a position of perennial hurt. This reinforces something very unhelpful: passivity. Even with all our doing, hyperfunctioning, hypervigilance and attempts to rescue and control, ultimately, we believe ourselves to be victims and can relate to the world from this powerless place. We can be martyrs and struggle to take responsibility for ourselves. We neglect ourselves, ignore our self-care and can blame our partners or loved ones. We have a problem for every solution. We believe our struggles are very unusual and no one else understands.

Again, this heralds from our childhood, when we truly were powerless and often were the victim of an invalidating and inconsistent environment. As adults, we need to be careful that our very identity does not become the victim in every scenario. If we're not careful we will continue to perpetuate these patterns in our present-day relationships. We need to develop a new attitude and understanding of healthy attachment and what love is. We will learn about being accountable in Chapter 6.

Overcoming an anxiously attached state means committing to thinking in new ways that will reduce our anxiety, right-size our problems, and increase our independence and self-esteem. The more we repeat these and remind ourselves of these perspectives, slowly, over time, they will become our new beliefs around attachment. This is not a quick fix; it requires daily actions and discipline. However, it is absolutely possible and truly transformative. The solutions in Part III will help you to start making those changes.

Being secure does not mean being happy all the time or not having any problems. Being secure means bringing balance in our perspective, having a healthy mindset and attitude, and being able to look after ourselves and remain calm and adult in our interactions.

Nine steps to challenge anxious attachment

Becoming more secure requires ongoing, committed work. These steps outline what to focus on:

Step 1: Recognise our anxiously attached beliefs and behaviours.

Step 2: Recognise we are hyperfocused on the relationship and that that is part of the problem.

Step 3: Learn to emotionally regulate so we can tolerate the discomfort of silence, space and separateness (see Chapter 7).

Step 4: Seek reassurance and make it count, recognising all the ways it's communicated.

Step 5: Recognise our thinking is often fear-based and we are at the mercy of our feelings and story.

Step 6: Know your automatic responses and take responsibility by doing things differently.

Step 7: Work on communicating with dignity and composure (see Chapter 9).

Step 8: Recognise incompatibility and bad behaviour, and see what kind of a relationship is on offer with our partners, and if that is right for us.

Step 9 (ongoing): Continue to consciously shift from anxious to secure behaviours.

Journalling prompts

- Which patterns or traits as described in this chapter are most relevant to you?
- Can you think of instances when this behaviour has negatively impacted your relationships, your friendships and/or your self-esteem? What were they?
- Can you recognise the origin of some of these patterns from your childhood and previous relationships? Describe.
- Are you able to bring compassion to yourself, understanding how and why you've had these experiences? Do you need to work on your self-compassion? Why might it be hard for you?
- Do you feel willing to work on breaking these patterns? What might be holding you back?

CHAPTER 4

Avoidant Attachment Traits and Tendencies – Dismissive and Fearful Avoidant

For those of us who are generally avoidantly attached in our relationships, we are aware of our lack of feelings and sometimes our lack of remorse or empathy. And in moments of deep fear, we worry we might be incapable of feeling.

In truth, being emotionless is to be expected if the messages we received while we were growing up – whether it was from our parents, caregivers, teachers, friends, culture or society – were don't cry, keep your thoughts and feelings to yourself, don't be vulnerable, be strong, suck it up, you're making a fuss, you're being difficult, no one cares, and on and on . . . Most of us – wisely – will have cut off from our emotional selves because otherwise we would be overcome with anguish. Bring in the numbing agents of social media, pornography, alcohol and drugs, addictions and myriad acting out behaviours and we're spoilt for choice on how to facilitate this ongoing dissociation.

To further complicate things, when we are avoidantly attached, it can be a *desirable* space for us to be in. We can feel very powerful, safe and protected – untouchable, even. In such a disappointing world this is our preferred stance. But those quieter moments when we think we might be lacking emotion entirely and possibly missing the point of life show us we are not entirely happy with this state of being. We can scare ourselves with our negative thoughts and almost existential apathy.

Charlie would sit in his bedroom staring at his phone. Having just had an argument with his partner, he did what he routinely did, which was storm angrily out of the living room and go to the bedroom. He was fed up with his partner, who he felt was constantly criticising him. He didn't know what more he could do for her – her complaining was irritating and, more importantly, not true. Her accusing him of being unsupportive and not interested in her life was ridiculous. They'd just come back from visiting her annoying friend Jess!

Their fights were getting worse and worse and Charlie hated her negative attitude and retreated further into himself with every altercation, feeling nothing but disdain towards her. He wasn't interested in 'talking things through', as she kept nagging him to do - he just wanted peace and quiet. 'This relationship isn't working out,' he thought. 'I don't need this kind of stress in my life. This is her problem, not mine.'

Deep down, we all want something else. Love is not the cherry on the cake. Love is a primal, crucial need – a biological driver. And when, somewhere along the line, love became too overwhelming or too dangerous for us to engage in, that was a huge loss. A loss that could last forever. So, if in a tortured moment you have thought you might be an automaton, let's really use that and do some self-work. This may not feel natural, it may not even feel good, but it's a muscle we need to develop if we want to experience what it means to be truly alive – and a feeling human being.

If we are resistant to investing in our relationships then there is very little to sustain them and they can fizzle out. How do we keep the fun and passion, communication and connectedness going when we actively avoid it? Even relationships that have that exciting spark, and could well have everything we want to go the distance, will flatline without our input. Or, our relationships become a huge source of dissatisfaction, we feel disconnected and this unsatisfying status quo becomes normalised.

You deserve significantly more than that.

In this chapter, we start by looking at general avoidant traits and behaviours, followed by an equally thorough exploration of dismissive avoidant and fearful avoidant traits. There will be crossovers and similarities between these two types of avoidance, but it's useful to see the hallmarks of both in order to ask which correspond with you and your relational beliefs. Consider all the sections as you will likely be familiar with behaviours from them all. This is to be expected – we naturally develop many different ways to defend ourselves and keep ourselves safe in relationships. What we recognise highlights where we need to focus our efforts to learn and grow, so we may be more secure.

What we feel when we are avoidantly attached

These are some of the behavioural and emotional experiences that can occur when we are avoidantly attached:

- Frustrated we're not getting the space or time alone that we need.

- Apathetic because we are disconnected from our feelings.
- Feeling micromanaged or controlled when people want us to make plans in advance.
- Socially awkward because we don't know what to say.
- Powerful as we withhold from talking, calling, messaging or engaging with others at all.
- Scathing of people who fall in love easily.
- Smothered when others want us to be affectionate.
- Isolated as we struggle to ask for help.
- Emotionless during sex or only focused on our orgasm.
- Zoning out of difficult conversations or situations.
- Stressed when our partners approach us wanting to connect.
- Content and free when alone.
- Fed up and hassled by other people's needs.
- Repelled by the emotional messiness of relationships.
- Dodging taking responsibility.
- Invulnerable as we wall ourselves off.
- Tranquilising ourselves with numbing-out behaviours.
- Empty in times of loneliness.

These are some of the coping strategies we may use when avoidantly attached:

- withdrawing
- having time and space alone
- regulating our emotions with activities or projects
- demonising our partners

- hating others
- fantasising about leaving the relationship
- making plans to leave the relationship
- becoming less inclined to work on things
- being scornful of working on the relationship
- rarely saying yes
- controlling our partners with silence and disapproval
- overfocusing on our partners' failings
- shutting down and pushing people away
- numbing out with work, alcohol, drugs or something else
- isolating as a way of protecting ourselves

Avoidant Traits

Below, you'll see avoidant ways of relating that you might recognise when you are in conflict, upset or angry. These are the behavioural patterns and processes that perpetuate our insecure ways of relating and will maintain our avoidance. Some may not be relevant to you, or different reactions may occur at different times, with different relationships. The chapters in Part III will give you the tools to shift away from these unhelpful behaviours, so you can experience more peace and contentment in your partnerships.

Shutting down

The shutting down that is part of the avoidant process is probably one of the hardest to challenge. Shutting down is a deeply primitive coping strategy and it's very effective. Not feeling anything, which we can mistake for not caring for the other person, is a very reassuring place to be. We are back in control, we feel powerful and we are undisturbed by the messy workings of relationships.

So, this supremely comfortable place is a difficult thing to relinquish. Why would we forfeit such a glorious situation in which we are unburdened by what others think of us, the requirements of commitments or, most notably, the need to look inwards and reflect on our own unhappiness or unhelpful behaviour? It is precisely this kind of personal responsibility that we avoid. We don't know how to do it and we don't believe we need to do it.

Part of our avoidance is about avoiding ourselves too. Generally, we are disconnected from ourselves, unaware of what we are feeling (believing instead that what we think is what we feel), lacking insight into ourselves. Because of the shutting down that was required of us in order to feel safe when we were younger, we sadly closed ourselves off in every respect.

Alone time is important. It's physical, mental, emotional, psychological space from a life that can feel overly stimulating sometimes. Taking space (and being allowed to take space) is ultimately a good thing because we can come back to our lives with more resource. We feel rested, clearer, willing and wanting to be part of life and relationships again. Avoidance is different. We can get stuck here – we're not taking space, we're shutting down. When we withdraw, it can be a reactive, numbing out, dissociative action. It is primal; the flight of the survival response. Distinguishing between taking time for ourselves and avoidance is our work.

Avoiding messy feelings

We are not keen on feelings. The whole point of avoidance is to postpone feeling (ideally forever). Who wants to feel miserable? Processing and metabolising big emotion is extremely taxing for us and, when the people around us are exhibiting extreme emotion, this is the surest trigger we have. While we may feel very strong in our avoidant state, the truth of the matter is we are not very robust. At best, we can be emotionally lazy; at worst, we can be emotionally absent.

We can work on gradually tolerating not only the emotions of those around us but also our own emotions, of which we are often unaware. As adults, we are able to withstand difficult emotions and we also have a great opportunity to begin embracing other emotions that are hard for us to experience, like joy, peace, excitement and fulfilment. Through the emotional regulation exercises outlined in Chapter 7 we can learn to tolerate exploring our emotions for small periods of time. We can be curious about how we might feel about subjects that we avoid or dismiss.

A big avoidant process is tranquilising feelings. We turn to processes and substances which facilitate our avoidance: work, exercise, drink, drugs, food, masturbation, pornography, sex, fantasy are all very effective at anaesthetising us and helping us believe we are 'fine'. Depending on how entrenched and habituated these behaviours are, we can reflect on how this might be impacting our lives and especially our relationships. If we are sleepwalking our way through our partnerships, we are missing out on so much.

Making bad choices in partners

Who do you keep choosing? Chances are, just like everyone else, you are drawn to people who will fulfil your expectations – not what you *want* but what your life experiences have taught you to expect from other people. With that in mind, you need to be aware of two things. First, who you are choosing and why, and second, how you relate to people.

Because our brains like order and making sense of things, we are quick to categorise people and relationships without necessarily getting the full information. That means we can be prone to projection, which is attributing qualities to the people around us that are based on our assumptions and expectations. And once we've projected what we expect on to others, relationships lose a lot of nuance and uniqueness.

We can consider our relationship history and reflect on whether our people-picker could do with adjusting. If we're naturally choosing people with whom a certain kind of unhealthy relationship is inevitable, that is really something to notice (look back at the exercise in Chapter 2 and see what you uncovered). Who we choose to have in our life is very important and we might need to bring more intentionality to our choices and be open to new and different people.

It is not random who ends up in our life. We are making choices and we need to take responsibility for those choices. When we are avoidantly attached that tells us that what is familiar to us isn't always healthy because we've had to develop a way of dealing with relationships that results in us checking out. So the people we choose may end up behaving in ways we've come to expect: they want too much from us. That might include people who are more focused on themselves and their own needs, or people who are overwhelming to our nervous systems. This is one of the biggest reinforcers of all our patterns: choosing people who we need to continually defend ourselves against.

But not always. It's sometimes difficult for us to recognise when someone is having appropriate requirements from us in relationships as we will respond to most requests as demands and, when very triggered, may feel giving anything at all is too much.

We need to reflect on what are bad choices that are sabotaging our efforts to move forward and what is us projecting on others the behaviour we expect.

When we are in a defensive position, we are not seeing clearly. As we look after ourselves with boundaries (see

Chapter 10), we can begin relating to people more authentically, and choosing partners who can be healthy and loving, so we are not destined to repeat old hurts and engage in relationships that are not good for us.

Bad choices versus projecting what we expect

Learning to distinguish between unhealthy choices that will harm us and our fears and projections that may be sabotaging our happiness is vital. Consider the below for clarity:

Bad choices:

- Ignoring incompatibilities and focusing on externals (looks, status, money).
- Choosing people who are highly emotive or even unstable.
- Believing someone will change/not accepting what someone is showing you.
- Feeling put down and criticised constantly but still staying.

Projecting:

- Making sweeping statements and jumping to conclusions during conflict.
- Ignoring kind, positive and caring behaviour.
- Being obstructive, vague and doing the bare minimum and then feeling vindicated when our partners react with upset.
- Judging people quickly then pigeonholing them into familiar categories.

Lack of awareness about our ways of relating and behaving

Sometimes we can lack awareness about our own behaviour and the likely responses that behaviour will evoke. One of the main aims of this book is to help you develop insight into what we do and identify the ways of relating that may be getting in the way of achieving our goals. So much of our behaviour is inherently defensive, which is a way of engaging with others when we're stressed that can be combative, or perceived as combative. We might feel we are simply stating our needs and keeping ourselves safe, while our partners and family might feel that they are being put down or actively fought.

We can be very good at condemning the behaviour of the people around us but it's important we turn our analysis to ourselves. What are *we* doing to contribute to our less-than-ideal circumstances? We can examine:

- our attitude
- the tone we take with people
- our belief systems and history (as explored in chapters 1 and 2)
- how easy it is for us to forgive
- how compassionate we can be

All of these need to be addressed if we are to be mature adults who can contribute to our lives and the lives of those we love.

Emotionally self-sufficient to the point of isolating

A great gift of relationships is having someone to do life with, but that also means having someone else to take into consideration. When we are avoidant, this can be alarming to us. In our self-sufficiency, we are happy looking after ourselves, going about our lives, and we can feel very uneasy when other people rely on us or want too much from us. Yet relationships mean more of a team mentality than in our singular lives. What might be best for us may not be best for the team; what makes us happy may not be great for the relationship. In order for our relationship to thrive, it's going to require efforts from us that are often uncomfortable. How we love one another matters, and that includes learning how to take someone else into account and to actively make their life a little bit better with our presence in it.

To begin letting people into our lives more, we can reach out to others and invite them in to offer support and assistance. We can push ourselves to be slightly more social and, when we do so, share a little bit more of ourselves: tell stories, share our thoughts and push ourselves beyond what we would normally share.

How to reach out to others in small, achievable ways

- Invite someone to join you in an activity you normally do alone (going for a walk, grocery shopping or even playing video games/watching a show).
- Challenge yourself to make three ten-minute calls a week to friends and family and be as open about yourself as you can for those ten minutes.
- When questioning something in your life, ask someone for advice or their opinion.

- Develop your capacity for small talk by exchanging a few words with someone at the bus stop/a work meeting/ the checkout.
- Don't automatically assume you've got to do everything yourself. When faced with a task, consider asking someone to lend a hand.

Attachments are disappointing

Relationships are very challenging, there's no doubt about that. However, if we believe that relationships are inevitably going to be disappointing, we are never going to truly open our hearts to any possibility other than this. We are doing ourselves a significant disservice, however understandably, because how do we experience something different when we think we know how everything is going to turn out anyway? We can be hypervigilant to the negative in our partners and relationships – this is our way of protecting ourselves from these inevitable disappointments. We use each new experience as proof that our stance of avoidance is justified and indeed sensible. Why trust other people when we are the only trustworthy ones we know?

Look to your friendships and outside relationships for proof of the contentment that is possible in partnerships. You might notice the benefits of having people in your life: companionship, enjoyment and fun, having someone to support you during tough times and vice versa, sharing memories and making plans.

Ask yourself if you are willing to risk some pain in order to arrive at something potentially fulfilling. Our nervous systems are too sensitive to the challenges of relationships and we need to develop our robustness. As we'll explore in

Part III, we *can* cope with difficulty, we *can* handle tough conversations and we *can* open our hearts to include other people in our lives. These are micro-risks worth taking, which we can consciously and intentionally choose to do as we go about our lives. Relationships are what *we* make them.

Hyper-focused on our partners' perceived failings

This is an incredibly powerful, and very compelling, process. The minute we experience anger, vulnerability, hurt, fear or suspicion, our avoidance will turn our laser-sharp focus on to our partners and their perceived failings. This creates the distance that we need between ourselves and what we believe is the source of our disturbance. And because we hold ourselves in high regard, and believe our life is simple and easy when we are unencumbered, we can be very quick to blame and demonise our partners when we are confronted with relational difficulty, no matter how great or small.

This is a difficult behaviour to pin down, as we feel so justified in our thoughts and opinions, not realising that the purpose of these thought processes is to separate us from our loved ones and entrench our avoidance even further.

A key factor to adult relationships is problem-solving. When people come together, two or more worlds are colliding. Everyone will have their own preferences, thoughts, opinions, hopes and dreams, and all of that lands on the relationship to somehow be fulfilled. If the first line of defence is to demonise our partners, it is very difficult to stay motivated towards the often painful and unpleasant process of working things out together. This is where a boundary needs to be put in place, whereby we do not allow ourselves to get too negative in our own minds about our partners.

Developing respect for the people we love is important work (see Chapter 9 for advice on this). Being avoidant means that we are quick to disrespect others and this is where we can get stuck.

> We need to nurture respect. Due to our childhood and early life experiences, often we do not have respect for other people and this is carried over into our partnerships.

Mental and emotional dissociation

'I'm fine' may be what we mistakenly believe about our emotional and mental state a lot of the time, but the truth of the matter is we may be dissociated from the thoughts and feelings we are experiencing. Depending on how extreme our avoidant coping strategies are, we can shut down very easily. We might disappear into our own world, feel like we are outside ourselves looking in, and sometimes have no recollection of certain conversations or situations. These are signs of dissociation, or derealisation or depersonalisation, which are anxious responses but are avoidant in nature. Often starting in our childhood, we check out of challenging situations, which can herald the beginning of a lifelong struggle with staying emotionally present in real-life moments.

The nature of dissociating means that we don't realise it's happening. And then we don't remember once we've done it. If you know you can disappear into your own head, or friends and loved ones have remarked on you 'not being there', or you can't remember conversations or interactions, this can alert you to the possibility this may be happening for you. You can then reflect on the situations that evoke the dissociative response in you. What is going on that feels stressful or overwhelming? Why might it feel dangerous in some way for you? Why is there a need for you to run for the hills, metaphorically speaking?

Then, we can work on staying grounded in certain conversations, slowing things down and considering the boundaries we need in order to stay as present as possible. We'll cover all this and more in chapters 7, 9, and 10.

Struggling to be verbal or consistently stay in touch

Not only are we often not talkers, especially on intimate and deep subjects, we can also be people who don't keep in touch. Messages are often sporadic, monosyllabic or supremely brief. While this may not be a problem, being inconsistent and, at times, rude is. We might believe in brevity but those around us – often family and loved ones – want more from us. And this is where our automatic responses come in. We like to give the bare minimum to others so that the bare minimum is expected from us. We can desensitise to staying in touch, silencing any judgements we might have about it.

It is these sorts of unhelpful associations with relationships that we are trying to challenge, because relationships by their very nature involve people caring for us, wanting to know about us and wanting us to care about them. This is not something that comes naturally to us and we therefore sometimes have to recognise that, although we do not require chatty messages or prompt responses, other people do. When we love people, it means going out of our way sometimes to take their feelings into consideration and, where we can, demonstrating our love overtly. We can experiment with more affectionate language and commit to, if nothing else, being consistent. Chapter 9 will outline more on this, guiding you to some simple, easy wins.

Consistency is an excellent goal for those of us with avoidant issues, as we can take responsibility for the way in which we show up for people and, if we want others to be secure as well, we can know that consistency is a key contributor to that.

Trust issues

We don't really trust anyone except ourselves. We have become self-reliant for a reason and, many moons ago, stopped relying on others. However, this can cause problems in our love lives as our partners want to get close to us and be intimate with us. This requires things we do not like: vulnerability and trust. It's daunting for most people and, for us, it can feel doubly so. All of our safety-making mechanisms are about being self-sufficient and self-reliant. We do not open ourselves up to others. That is how we stay safe.

Letting people into our hearts is not an overnight exercise and we do not have to make ourselves too vulnerable too quickly. But we do need to challenge ourselves to take those risks as our relationships develop and appropriate closeness increases. People can earn our trust but we need to be open to the possibility for this to happen (how to develop trust appropriately is covered in Chapter 8). A lot of the time, the shutters are down, and it doesn't matter how kind and loving someone is to us, we won't open up to them. To challenge this, we can choose when and how much we give ourselves to the people we feel as safe as we possibly can with.

However, we must be careful we don't overcorrect after we've been vulnerable. We need to watch out that we do not become defensive after having shared with someone. Sometimes, after we have been vulnerable, we can retreat even further or overcompensate with distancing behaviours, like picking fights, fault-finding and needing to assume the one-up position again. Feeling exposed, we can unconsciously want to take back power and our avoidant coping mechanisms will come out in full force.

Assertiveness

We might think we are assertive but from a relational point of view, we are perhaps being aggressive or obstructive. Assertiveness has respect to it. We are respecting ourselves but we are communicating in a way that respects the other person too. We do not have to like people or even condone what they are doing, but we can speak to them in ways we would like to be spoken to. This is what secure adults do. Because sometimes we can get bent out of shape when people communicate to us in ways we find displeasing, can't we? We can fall into the trap of speaking to others in ways we would never tolerate or accept, and certainly not feel good about, if the roles were reversed. Not only do we deserve to feel respected in our interactions but we can develop our self-esteem so we treat others with dignity too.

We might pride ourselves on our firmness and directness, and not lowering ourselves to other people's verbose ways, but this can be avoidant. Communication encompasses so much – the expression on our faces, language, the cadence of our voice, what we say and how we say it. Being passive or aggressive may feel natural but, ultimately, it is not constructive or esteeming. Assertiveness is emotionally intelligent and responsible; it is what will yield the best results and also enrich our relationships (and relational skills). This is all covered in Chapter 9.

Fear of being engulfed

For many of us, there is an unconscious process at play where we fear being taken over by our partners and their needs. We may not have memories of this but there could have been a time in our childhood when our caregiver was more focused on their own needs than ours and perhaps looked to us as a way of meeting their needs. We can often be drafted in by our parents/caregivers into overly responsible relationships that shift the dynamics and interrupt their caregiving to us. It is natural for the child to go to their caregiver for comfort and help, not the other way round. When our caregivers lean on us, that changes the roles of everyone involved. There can be different degrees of this, from subtle and minimal to overt parentification. This would have been too much for us (whether we realised it or not) and can leave us with a resistance to getting too close to people later in life because other people overwhelm us with their stuff.

It was not appropriate for us to be leaned on when we were younger as we grew up and, fortunately, our adult relationships are very different. It is appropriate to be interdependent in our partnerships, to go to people for support and to let them support us. But because of our experiences when we were younger, these appropriate requirements of relationships today can often feel like outrageous demands on our very self.

It would be helpful to desensitise to the natural interconnectedness in relationships, allowing our nervous system to discover that we can withstand appropriate connection and that people are not out to overwhelm or overpower us.

By learning how to be close with our partners, and by making sure we are not engulfed through healthy boundaries, we can open ourselves up a little bit to people who have earned our trust and who we know have our well-being at the forefront of their minds. The whole of this book, but especially Part III, is dedicated to helping you achieve exactly that.

Need to have control

Many of us need to own up to our need to have control in our relationships. If we were to ask the people in our life if they found us controlling at times, what would they say? This is something for us to work on. Sometimes our controlling behaviour is overt: telling people what to do, being overly critical, and making hurtful and disparaging comments when they behave in ways that we don't like, and even punishing our partners. Or it can be covert: controlling the atmosphere of a relationship with our disapproval or anger, setting up our partners to fail and subtly putting them down.

We can exert healthy control in our lives. Learning what is appropriate, and what is unhealthy and unpleasantly dominating, is what we can explore. We certainly do not like to feel controlled and we can endeavour not to do it to people we care about.

Merging sex and love

Sex is often just sex for us. It is a release, a physical act, and it can be devoid of emotion and also love. Even when we do love someone, the sexual act is often just that – an action. This means that we can be in danger of having emotionless sex, of thinking only of our needs during sex and of being disconnected or insensitive.

Merging ideas of sex with ideas of love can allow our bodies and hearts to experience a more relational embodiment of love: tenderness, affection, pleasure and another person's pleasure, a feeling of togetherness. This is what intimacy is all about: connecting in deeper and more meaningful ways.

When we believe we love someone, we can choose to demonstrate that in physical and sexual ways. We can be mindful of their preferences and experience, and take time and effort to please them, relax them and make them feel important. We can also stop viewing sex as something that is primarily about, and concludes with, our orgasm. Connected sex isn't about what we're thinking in our heads, it's about what we're feeling in our bodies and what we are noticing in the body we are being intimate with. If we want it to be, this could be very enjoyable indeed.

Nine steps to challenge avoidant attachment

Step 1: Recognise our avoidantly attached beliefs and behaviours.

Step 2: Recognise that we close ourselves off from people and that that is part of the problem.

Step 3: Learn to emotionally regulate so we can tolerate the connectivity relationships sometimes require (see Chapter 7).

Step 4: Learn to meet our needs of autonomy and space without abandoning our partners or relationships.

Step 5: Recognise that our thinking is often fear-based and that we are at the mercy of our rationality and negativity.

Step 6: Know our automatic responses and take responsibility by doing things differently.

Step 7: Work on communicating with respect and openness (see Chapter 9).

Step 8: Recognise incompatibility and bad behaviour, and see what kind of a relationship is on offer with our partners, and if that is right for us.

Step 9 (ongoing): Continue to consciously shift from avoidant to secure behaviours.

Dismissive Avoidant Traits

When our dismissive avoidant attachment is activated, our view of relationships changes. We can shut down and be emotionless about relationships and the people in our life, and we can fall into a devaluing and dismissive mindset about people and relationships as a way of keeping people at arm's length and feeling more in control and separate.

'It's the put-downs!' Riley's partner would cry. During times of conflict, Riley would 'armour up' and, after initially nonchalant behaviour, like shrugging, silence and staring off into the distance, could savage her partner or whoever was trying to speak to her. Serious conversation was scorned and derided, and Riley's partner didn't know how to get through to her. The shutters would come down for Riley and there was no penetrating them; she seemed so cold and indifferent, making everyone walk on eggshells or totally back off.

What we feel when we are dismissively attached

These are some of the behavioural and emotional experiences that can occur when we are dismissively attached:

- Scathing of other people and their neediness.
- Superiority as we judge others.
- Boredom when engaging in serious or long conversations.
- Inflexible: will only do things when we want, how we want.
- Self-righteous: we are rude to people in the name of being 'honest'.
- Put off when someone does something that annoys us or we don't like.
- Resolute as we flip the switch and turn off our feelings.
- Pleased with ourselves/grandiose.
- Unbothered by what other people think of us.

- Easily irritated or offended.
- Furious and needing to leave whatever and whoever is upsetting us.
- Indignant as we criticise and character assassinate our partners, blaming them for everything.
- Dismissive of our own emotional experiences (like sadness or vulnerability).

Dismissive avoidant coping strategies:

- Judging others while elevating ourselves.
- Avoiding closeness or intimate communication.
- Shutting down to regulate our emotions (dissociating).
- Focusing on blame and demonising our partners.
- Abandoning our partners.
- Acting grandiose and assuming the one-up position.
- Being overly rational and rigid in our attitudes.
- Putting up impenetrable walls.
- Being critical and unkind in our communication.
- Devaluing people and relationships.
- Controlling our partners with disapproval.

Minimising the importance of relationships

We have many things that matter to us in our lives: work and careers, projects we believe in, life philosophies we hold dear, a clear purpose or a devotion to spiritual or political pursuits. We don't have a problem with prioritising these aspects of our life; we value them and, therefore, we naturally make time and space for them. What is less easy for us is to allow relationships to be supremely important to us too.

We may like having relationships, we might enjoy having people in our lives, but somehow they do not matter as much as many other things do.

We can devalue others, which is revealed through our thoughts and beliefs, like: 'They aren't so great', 'They're annoying', 'I don't need this/anyone', 'I just want to be on my own', 'Hell is other people', and so on.

The first step in breaking this habit is to stop diminishing relationships in your mind. Check your attitude. Are you positive about relationships? About any of your relationships or other people's? Or do you openly (or secretly) mock relationships, especially people who value them? In doing this, you continue to programme yourself deeper into your avoidance. And because you are dismissive, there is a very sharp edge to your views. This is a big habit to break. Catch yourself being negative, take responsibility for turning the volume down on the negative commentary you have about other people and their relationships. Tools for this are explored in Chapter 8.

Judging others for having needs

Our way of feeling strong and powerful in our relationships is to be scathing towards others – it helps us feel safe because we put ourselves in a one-up position by putting everyone else around us down. This is a very powerful shield and one we don't want to give up because it gives us the illusion of strength and invulnerability. Actually, it can be very sad as people we love and care about end up feeling bad about themselves and walk on eggshells around us, and we become known as the rude/unkind/temperamental/difficult one. It's easy for us to be scornful of other people who are open about their need for other people, validation and affection. To us, this is the ultimate weakness.

Or is it? How satisfied are *we* in our hearts of hearts?

How passionate are our lives in and outside our bedrooms? When was the last time we experienced joy with another human being? These are all part of a full life but they belong in the emotive world. Some of us are prepared to sacrifice all of that to live on our remote islands.

Having needs is natural. Wanting things from other people does not make us clingy. People wanting something from us does not have to mean there's a problem. By being judgemental of others, we demonise simple, basic human connection.

Boundaries (covered in Chapter 10) are our friends because we do not have to be totally open, 24/7, to other people. By putting boundaries in place with others we can reduce the possibility of being overwhelmed by their needs and, if we have boundaries with ourselves, we can make sure we don't get too negative in our thinking or isolate for too long. We can keep our interactions manageable for ourselves. By putting in effort to step fully into the parts of life that involve other people, we can realise just how easily we can cope and that it is not as awful as our belief system will make us believe.

How to move away from being judgemental and critical

You have probably spent an awful lot of time training your brain towards the negative. Being critical is your first and most alluring reaction. You therefore need to rewire your brain towards something much more relational: appreciation, understanding and giving credit where credit is due.

Set yourself some challenges:

- Give the people in your life at least one compliment a day.
- In a quiet moment, sit down and think about your day or your week and, rather than considering all the things that went wrong, or your partner's failings or incompetence, or how everyone around you annoyed you, instead, look for the things that went right.
- Think about what's going on for the people around you and how life might feel from their perspective.
- Think of things your partner did that were admirable, kind or attractive. Think of the traits you like about your friends and loved ones, and what you can spend a little bit more time enjoying and appreciating.

What we focus on expands. As long as we focus on all the flaws and failings of those around us, those flaws will become disproportionately large and dominate our perspective, which will make it very hard for them - and us - to succeed.

Dismissing our emotions

We don't only dismiss others, we dismiss our own emotional experiences too. Contrary to what we might believe, we are not automatons and bulletproof; we are constantly having emotional reactions to our lives and, depending on how connected we are to those parts of ourself, we can dismiss or avoid the difficult stuff.

With dismissiveness, when we shame others for their

emotional reactions, we also reinforce our own avoidance. We believe our own judgements and don't allow ourselves emotional experiences. Over time, if our defences have repeatedly prioritised protecting ourselves from uncomfortable or unpleasant emotions, we can become completely disconnected. Emotions do not go quietly, however. When we are shut-down our emotions present themselves in other ways: impulsive and compulsive behaviour, physical ailments, mental health issues like depressive episodes or anxiety, relationship problems and employment issues speak of our pain and upset coming out sideways.

We are not machines. Our feelings are there, and we need to build a relationship with them that is friendlier and more compassionate (see Chapter 7 for more on this).

Being unreliable

Having learnt to rely only on ourselves can mean we have become unreasonably unreliable to others by not making plans, committing ourselves or turning up for social occasions. Being unreliable might keep other people's expectations of us very low but it also means we miss out on the satisfying aspects of being human – being a member of a group, helping others and being a valued and important part of our families, friendship circles and communities.

Commit to something that pushes you out of your comfort zone: do volunteer work, offer your services at the next family party or get-together, check in with friends and family to see if they need help or support with anything. As you put yourself out in the world, you will discover how rewarding it is to be there for the people in your life, to turn up for them in ways that have meaning for both you and them. We can desensitise to people relying on us and, rather than it being an unwanted demand and drain, we realise that a little bit of discomfort is tolerable as we become part of the human race, and understand the meaning of the words 'partnership' and 'team'.

Fault-finding

Is it very easy for you to be mean-spirited or make 'funny', caustic comments? Are you generally able to find fault with someone or something? And is it difficult for you to be generous, patient and understanding? If that is the case, your dismissiveness may have taken over.

This is something of a default position for us. When we are unhappy or displeased, we over-focus on the relationship and become fixated on our partners' 'faults'. We can be supremely critical and unforgiving, and this perpetuates our dismissiveness. When we are fault-finding we are living in a negative distorted reality but our insecure attachment tells us it's truth.

It's very easy to see when fault-finding has been normalised as a way of communicating because the complaints and criticism have become a constant refrain. When we are annoyed, we can't resist the snipes and jibes, the unpleasant comments and the sarcasm. This way of expressing ourselves is tragically compelling and can so easily become a habit – once we've started doing it, it seems quite difficult to stop.

The data clearly states that the contempt and criticism that is part and parcel of fault-finding is the final death knell of any relationship.

Having grandiose thoughts

Having felt very powerless in our lives, we can relish the power grandiose thoughts and behaviours can afford us now. But these are illusions and continue the pattern of distancing people from us, rubbing people up the wrong way and keeping ourselves isolated and alone.

Our avoidance is not borne from a superior position or stronger character. Rather, it is our way of responding to devastating attachment wounding and part of some very lonely-making ways of keeping ourselves safe.

Notice how quickly you can go into scornful or a moral-high-ground way of speaking and relating. For example, 'They're pathetic', 'She's got problems' or 'How can you be so stupid?' This is grandiosity. Underneath are real fears about relationships that need to be tackled. As long as we are grandiose, we hide behind walls of superiority, when, in fact, what I observe in my clients is that what we really feel is very lost and confused. We are tired of feeling empty in our relationships. We deserve meaningful and enriching relationships as much as anyone else, so learning how to stay equal to others and not choose an inflated sense of self over a real connection with another person is imperative.

Rejecting other people's opinions and thoughts

Is it fair to say that sometimes, we – especially when hurt, angry or upset – aren't the most open-minded, generous-spirited, curious-about-other-people's-thoughts-and-opinions kind of people? That we're more 'It's my way or the high-way' kind of people instead?

It's admirable to be strong-willed and to know our own minds. However, we can also be inflexible in our thinking. Taking it even further, we can be intolerant of others and, if we don't agree with what they are saying, we dismiss it (and them) as completely irrelevant. Relationally, it can be difficult for us to have empathy for our partners or take them into account. If they express things we don't agree with or under-stand, we can put them down in the most crushing ways and, in the extreme, we can mock and character assassinate. These aren't great characteristics. And they are certainly not going to nurture tender and warm relationships.

Maybe it's quite nice to think people tiptoe around you and are wary of you; it makes you feel strong. But is that ideal for a romantic partnership? Would it be so terrible to be accommodating, acknowledging that your partner will have their own thoughts and opinions – and not only is that allowed but preferable? Things like acceptance and tolerance are forgotten skills we need to bring back. We possibly did not get a lot of patience and understanding ourselves growing up, and so we did not learn these traits. But we can focus our efforts on getting them now. We can try to be a bit more human with those we love.

At the mercy of our negative, overly rational thinking

We are generally very cut off from our bodies and therefore our emotions and instincts, having long since disappeared into our heads, intensely rationalising and intellectualising most things. That logical approach to life stands us in good stead: things make sense, life feels ordered, we are in control. This all satisfies our need for security on a superficial level.

But being so logical also has some downsides. We miss nuance and we can lack other components relationships require, such as empathy, compassion and acceptance. We can be fixed on rationality, facts and what we think. This leaves huge holes in the shape of experience and feelings. Not a lot of our relational lives fits into organised boxes of logic and reason – when it involves our bodies and hearts, as well as our minds, there are many, many more shades of grey than we can sometimes appreciate.

When we are anxiously attached, we are at the mercy of our emotions. When we are avoidantly attached, we are at the mercy of our negative, overly rational thoughts. We can be very all-or-nothing in our views, buying into a right and wrong, good and bad mentality, which only serves to compound our inflexible rationales.

Instead, we can recognise that thoughts are not facts. We can acknowledge that they are subjective and will be influenced by all of our life's experiences, prejudices, fears and defences. What we think is not always our most reliable source. In fact, we can learn not to trust our thinking. We can start to recognise when we are being extreme in our thinking and strive to bring in balance. We can challenge ourselves, be curious about our thoughts, check in with our bodies, practise emotional regulation work (see Chapter 7) and begin to break down the hard barrier of our mental security gates. As unnerving as it might be to consider, just because we think something, does not make it so.

Nine steps to challenge dismissive avoidant attachment

Step 1: Recognise our dismissive avoidant attachment beliefs and behaviours.

Step 2: Recognise that we are hypercritical and that is a big part of the problem.

Step 3: Learn to emotionally regulate so we can tolerate the discomfort of learning to be equal with others (see Chapter 7).

Step 4: Challenge our relentless negativity towards, and devaluing of, others.

Step 5: Recognise that our thinking is often disrespectful and we are at the mercy of our rationality.

Step 6: Know our automatic responses and take responsibility by doing things differently.

Step 7: Work on communicating with respect (see Chapter 9).

Step 8: Recognise incompatibility and bad behaviour, and see what kind of a relationship is on offer with our partners, and if that is right for us.

Step 9 (ongoing): Continue to consciously shift from dismissively avoidant to secure behaviours.

Fearful Avoidant Traits

When our fearful avoidant attachment is activated, our relationship fears take over. We can become highly anxious and self-conscious and be very frightened about relationships and the people in our life. To manage this extreme anxiety, we can behave erratically and unpredictably as we struggle to bring together our two conflicting desires: to have relationships with others and to protect ourselves from others at all costs.

After exploring their relationship history, Simone realised that their relationships have always been drama-filled and full of highs and lows. And their long-term partnership now is just the same: high-conflict, argumentative, both drinking too much and being miserable a lot of the time. A crush at work was becoming dangerously close to developing into something and if Simone hadn't recently been diagnosed with depression and adult ADHD they would have left their partner by now. They needed to make a decision but felt too scared to leave their partner, who Simone now considered 'boring', so kept going out with friends and avoided taking responsibility.

What we feel when we are fearfully attached

These are some of the behavioural and emotional experiences that can occur when we are fearfully attached:

- Overwhelmed by relationships and commitment.
- Erratic feelings towards others, swinging from love to hate.
- Terror at being rejected or 'not good enough'.
- Highly anxious and self-conscious when interacting with others.
- Impulsively start and end relationships.
- Feel angry with our partners a lot of the time.
- Can easily go off people and shut off to them.
- Escalate conversations into conflict and drama.
- Stuck, not able to make a decision or move in any direction.
- Very frightened of intimacy and emotional closeness.
- Unpredictable ways of behaving, responding or relating (what attachment psychotherapists call 'disorganised attachment').
- Seek out dramatic and dysfunctional scenarios and relationships.
- Tranquilise feelings to cope – alcohol, drugs, risk-taking, porn, gaming, gambling.

Fearful avoidant coping strategies:

- Reassurance-seeking through attention, intensity and drama.
- Proximity-seeking (but then being so anxious, resulting in pushing people away).

- Not able (or wanting) to regulate.
- Idealising or denigrating our partners.
- Abandoning ourselves or our partners.
- Avoiding emotional intimacy or emotionally dumping.
- Being boundaryless – extreme behaviour and communication.
- Being unreliable and inconsistent.
- Being fun and charming or angry and hostile.
- Craving relationships but fearing them more.
- Trying to control ourselves and/or our partners.
- Overthinking everything, escalating anxiety.
- Catastrophising and anticipating abandonment.

Fearing uncertainty

When we feel alone in the world, uncertainty is pretty intolerable. And we probably experienced this while we were growing up – a lot of turmoil and not a lot of reassurance and comfort from those who were looking after us. Uncertainty is not good for our nervous systems, especially when we are young. Feeling the security of our caregivers' protection and their ability to manage their own emotions and approach life difficulties with composure and constructive problem-solving is what would have removed uncertainty. In its place, we could have developed trust. Trust that we are okay, trust that the people in charge will look after us, and trust that there are no problems that will overcome us. Unfortunately, that probably was not our experience.

As we've seen, our nervous system is still very primitive. When we perceive threats, we will react as if our very survival depends on it. So when we perceive uncertainty, this will activate our threat system and, if we do not have the conditioning that a stable home environment provided growing up, we will very easily slide into all the primal fear our biology dictates.

Uncertainty does not threaten our survival. Uncertainty as an adult represents life's inevitable difficulty. It is a part of living and not one that we can dodge. Personal situations and societal challenges are ever-changing, and the modern world is full of uncertainties – or at least, the certainty of difficulty.

We can nurture self-soothing skills, loving compassion towards ourselves and healthy attitudes, so we can begin to adjust to weathering life's storms without collapsing into avoidance or acting out our anxiety. Part III will show you how.

Relationships feel too difficult, whereas drama is easy

Maybe we don't spend much time having relationships or maybe the norm for us is short-term flings and torrid affairs that fizzle out as quickly as they started. Or maybe we go from relationship to relationship, where dysfunction is a staple. Whichever of these we do, we continue to swim in the shallows of the short-term or superficial, and developing relationships into true intimacy or long-term commitment is something we will ultimately avoid.

Drama is an avoidant strategy. As long as there's drama there's no danger of the relationship genuinely progressing, as progress asks things of us we weren't taught: responsibility, accountability, stability, closeness, maturity and commitment. In order to get the love and care we crave, we have to learn to tolerate the discomfort of allowing people into our lives and loving wholeheartedly. By engaging in drama, we are never learning about relationships and we won't find the safety we desperately need. Our nervous systems need to be rewired so that they accept that security is a positive thing, because a lack of security, aka excitement and chemistry, has not worked out so well for us in the past.

We can learn ways of dealing with the stress relationships represent to us; we can let go of drama as a high-octane way of keeping ourselves safe, and we can focus our efforts on more effective solutions to our problems and challenges (see Part III for more on this).

Our fear of rejection and abandonment is all-consuming

The sad truth is we've been rejected repeatedly already. Our childhoods were often death by a thousand abandoning cuts, as the people around us focused on other things, dealing with their own struggles. In this way, we've already endured the worst. But because of these experiences, the fear of abandonment is more of a fact than just a fear. We know abandonment and, because we were so young when we experienced it, this is a trauma that lives on in us. We are terrified of it and expect it, all at the same time. This is the fear that is at the root of so much of our behaviour in our adult relationships, and sometimes we can even unconsciously seek it out or make it happen.

Rejection and abandonment can be found in many places. It can be in the ending of relationships, in infidelity and betrayal, but it can also be experienced when we're kept waiting or our messages don't receive a response in good time. It can be felt when a date ends or when our partners leave for a work trip. We can experience it when our partners go out without us, when they drink or drug too much, or when they have attractive friends. Depending on our sensitivity, the threat of rejection can be keenly felt in many scenarios and situations. In this way, we are retraumatised over and over. This then becomes the motivation for much fear-based, unconscious behaviour, such as: being hypervigilant, over-working, having stressful relationships, participating in harmful activities or lifestyles, avoiding caring for ourselves properly, and keeping our nervous systems activated. When we are doing this, we are doing the worst. We are abandoning ourselves. Chapter 6 will talk you through the importance of self-care.

Avoiding intimacy by picking fights

Love and conflict can often be entwined in our minds. Having volatile disagreements with people we love is a big part of our story. Because of our anxiety around relation-ships, we can react into any version of fight, flight, freeze or fawn in an instant. And fight is often a firm favourite. Some-times it's a way of defending ourselves and just an automatic instinct; other times, it's a way of drawing people in, a way of connecting with people, but not authentically (like shar-ing vulnerably). And sometimes, when a situation requires intimacy, responsibility or honesty, we will pick fights as a way of avoiding because we lack the relational skills needed.

Ultimately, fighting is not constructive. It's something we do *instead* of being intimate with people. When intimacy develops, we become more frightened as there is nothing more dangerous for us than closeness.

Even though we might fear conflict and the possible abandonment that conflict can result in, our reactivity will be in charge and, because we imagine the worst, will (re)act first and ask questions later (if ever). This creates tension, ill-feeling and unhappiness, but also raised heartbeats and adrenaline spikes to which we may be addicted.

We have to take responsibility for managing our emo-tions better so we can slowly begin to learn how to share ourselves with others in ways that will maximise closeness and connection, not escalate conflicts. Learning the emotional regulation techniques and communication skills outlined in chapters 7 and 9 are what will truly help you to move forward.

Fear of intimacy

Intimacy disorders are a result of various experiences/ forms of trauma, and they impact our ability to attach to others because we have a fear of emotional or physical closeness with another person. Due to this, we avoid the intimacy of long-term committed relationships, connecting with others or being too vulnerable. At the same time, we are also very fearful of isolation and sexual deprivation, so our behaviour can become unhealthy and we act out in love addiction, sexual compulsions and addictive relationships. We can also feel stuck in relationships because progressing a relationship in the present day is a huge leap of faith - and the reality is, we don't have a lot of faith in people or ourselves.

However, when we are with a person we can, over time, assess and work out if they are someone with whom we can share a life. We can think about what we want from life now and in the long term. As leading relationship therapist and author Esther Perel says, 'People we love are not necessarily the same people we can make a life with. Life stories are not the same as love stories.'

We might be familiar with the excitement of thrilling entanglements, but we are not familiar enough with the reality of what sharing a contented life might look like. This is what we have to think through. Can we rely on people? Do they want the best for us? Do we respect each other? Can we be responsible together? These are questions we can ask ourselves when we're in relationships, allowing time and experience to inform their answers. This is how we create the security we need and make the best decisions for our future.

Feeling angry with others most of the time

Whether we realise it or not, there is a constant bell going off in us – a low-level state of irritability, anger or rage. We are grieving a whole life's painful experiences. Because of the destructive nature of our childhood and our early adulthood, it is natural for us to be in and out of numerous grief responses. We can be in shock, we can be in despair and we can be in various levels of rage. And we bring these states into all our present-day relationships and interactions. For many of us, it is not difficult for others to annoy us or to say the wrong thing to us. We are prickly and sensitive, reactive and antagonistic, accusatory and terrified. We might look angry on the outside but we feel very hurt on the inside.

We are stuck in anger because we haven't processed our grief and trauma, nor learnt to look after ourselves in loving and supportive ways. We're still fighting for our lives and, as long as we feel the need to do that, it will be very hard for us to live life peacefully and love others freely. We are in a constant state of survival mode, but we don't know how to do anything else because we've never really thought about our past and considered how it has impacted our lives, beliefs, perspective and self-esteem today. We need to focus on growing – emotionally and mentally – to take ourselves into account, to be responsible, to validate our life's experiences, acknowledge what has happened and how it still plays out today, so we can shift away from anger to determination, resolution, compassion and care.

I hope the tools and strategies in this book – particularly in Part III – can help you on your way. Deeper work in personal therapy can also be hugely transformative, as grief and trauma work is highly specialist. This could be time very well spent.

Defaulting to breaking up with people very quickly

As fearful avoidants, we have a dubious skill: our feelings can change in a heartbeat. We might like someone, really like someone, but if they say or do something that triggers us, the shutters can come down and, with a flick of a switch, we can go from liking them to loathing them. We can cut people out of our lives with staggering ease. When we're struggling with someone or experiencing some inevitable challenge in our love life or partnerships, we will either sabotage our relationships by creating the familiar atmosphere of problems and high conflict, or we get so scared and skittish when things may actually develop that we bolt for the door.

Sometimes, breaking up is what we need to do. If we are in a profoundly unhealthy relationship where it seems pain and difficulty is all that is on offer, we absolutely must walk away. However, we can also reflect on this powerful process where we end relationships impulsively – and end all growth and possibility at the same time.

When ending a relationship, we can feel temporarily happy but then become extremely depressed or low. Initially, there may be huge relief because relationships can feel excruciating, and as much as we want connection, at some point, our overwhelm is going to catch up with us. When we hit the eject button, we can feel a blessed release from all that exhausting anxiety and it gives us the false impression that breaking up with someone was the right thing to do. However, after a period of time, we can become depressed, question our choices and begin thinking we made a mistake. This is why our relationships can be full of make-ups and break-ups, and can be quite addictive.

When we do inevitably shut down to people, we can be aware that this is simply a coping strategy, and may not be a true reflection of our feelings and wishes. We can give ourselves time to think things through. We may question and reflect on what a more measured attitude would look like. We can temper hurt and angry feelings with the equally important fond and loving memories we have of people. We can lean into the messiness of relationships and their natural ups and downs. Every disappointment does not have to signify the end of the relationship.

Due to believing we're unlovable, we struggle to accept loving acts from other people

We don't really recognise love when we see it. We don't understand everyday kindnesses, acts of service and consistent ongoing affection, so when people in our lives try to offer us love we can struggle to accept it. We can even feel guilty or baffled. Some of us will think that there must be something wrong with someone else if they want to love us. We might also be in an unconsciously defensive position, not wanting anything from others lest we feel beholden. Or maybe we feel more comfortable caring for others and although probably wanting love, we are unable to let it in.

This speaks of the deprival we had in our past when many of our needs were unmet and many parts of us may have felt unloved. The great tragedy of this is that we often internalised a negative view of ourselves in the process: we learnt we are unlovable. In adulthood, these become our core beliefs about who we are and what we deserve. A huge shift for us is in realising we are truly worthy of love and these other life experiences were completely wrong and unjust.

We need to do the hard work of valuing ourselves possibly more than anyone else ever has. And we need to actively value different things in others: consistency, respect and accountability. We can learn to redefine what love is and, in particular, how lovable we are.

Yearning for people we believe we don't deserve

Oh, the agony of the romantic ruminating we do! We are fantasy addicts in a perennial state of yearning, wanting someone so much and believing, deep down, that we don't deserve such a prize. We don't grow out of crushes or get over bad break-ups. We can fixate and dream and obsess and stalk. From the youngest age, we probably yearned for our caregivers and family to look after us, to keep us safe and hold us. And that never leaves us. Despite being involved with so many other people throughout our lives, the hole in our soul can't seem to be filled. We weren't worthy of our caregivers' love growing up, so how could we imagine we would be worthy of anyone else's love now?

Can we bring compassion to the part of us that only ever wanted to be loved? That wanted to be validated and acknowledged by our caregivers, soothed and held? How deeply devastating that that was not our experience. The abandonment we experienced is something we internalised and continue to do to ourselves today. We still believe that some omnipotent being outside ourselves will heal us, love us enough, and we'll finally feel worthy.

Fortunately, relationships can be extremely healing – most notably our relationship with ourselves, which often requires time and attention. Once we learn how to care for ourselves in more meaningful ways (see Chapter 10), we can arrive in our relationships with so much more than yearning.

Nine steps to challenge fearful avoidant attachment

Step 1: Recognise our fearful avoidant attachment beliefs and behaviours.

Step 2: Recognise that, because of our anxiety, our behaviour becomes sabotaging and that that is what needs to be worked on.

Step 3: Learn to emotionally regulate so we can tolerate the discomfort of getting to know others slowly over time and intimacy increasing (see Chapter 7).

Step 4: Value moderation and balance; work towards achieving it in our relationships.

Step 5: Recognise that our thinking is often fear-based and that we are at the mercy of our dysregulated reactions.

Step 6: Know our automatic responses and take responsibility by doing things differently.

Step 7: Work on communicating with clarity and boundaries (see Chapter 9).

Step 8: Recognise incompatibility and bad behaviour, and see what kind of a relationship is on offer with our partners, and if that is right for us.

Step 9 (ongoing): Continue to consciously shift from fearfully avoidant to secure behaviours.

Avoidance eats time. Weeks, months, years can pass with no change or movement. And because we don't feel particularly unhappy in our avoidance, it can be effortful to challenge. To give ourselves the chance of experiencing something out-of-the-ordinary that will get under our walls, we have to open our hearts and do what feels extremely counter-intuitive: we need to learn to get close to people. Genuinely close.

Overcoming avoidant attachment means putting effort into reducing our defensive way of relating and developing new ways of engaging with others that is respectful, gentle and rooted in peace, not tension. It doesn't mean we stop being independent, that our lives get hijacked or we are constantly doing things we really don't want to do. It means we expand our repertoire to include other people more. We can come out of our castles or caves or islands and begin participating in life and relationships in ways that stretch us and warm our cool souls.

We can challenge the behaviours outlined above, we can bring awareness to what we automatically do, and we can practise more accountability to be available and adult in our interactions.

Long, long ago there was a young version of you that would have done anything to connect with your nearest and dearest. There's still time. Part III will help guide you towards the behaviours and adaptations that will reduce your avoidantly attached ways of relating.

Journalling prompts

- Which patterns and traits outlined in this chapter are most relevant to you?
- Can you think of examples when this behaviour has led to negative consequences?
- Can you recognise the origin of some of these patterns from your childhood and previous relationships? Describe.
- Do you feel willing to work on breaking these patterns? What might be holding you back?
- Write down the patterns you feel ready to address and do something about.

CHAPTER 5

What It Looks Like to Be Secure

The relationships our parents/caregivers had with each other (and certainly our grandparents' relationships) would surely be unrecognisable to the relationships we want and expect today. Long gone are the days of simply looking for security and companionship from our partnerships. We want life partners, co-parents, best friends, soulmates, twin flames, other halves and 'the one'. When my clients tell me something's missing from their relationship, it could be anything from a very long list. Never have we wanted more from each other.

The pursuit of these all-consuming, deep connections could be exciting and challenging; it could bring out our very best. However, there are other, hugely significant forces in our world: an environment of social media with a pervasive ideal of how perfect our lives need to be; sex and intimacy education via pornography; dating apps that promote a disposable attitude to relationships and people; and rising mental, emotional and sexual health issues.

We live in a world of anxiety, perfectionism and 'not enough'. And this is without doubt impacting our attitudes in our relationships. We want it all and we want it the way we want it. We expect nothing less. Whether we are aware of it or not, our expectations of ourselves and our relationships and our partners are sky high. And, as a result, we experience huge amounts of suffering and pain due to a continual sense of disappointment and being let down by others.

Our idea of love comes from some of our deepest and most unconscious beliefs. And it's when we explore the disillusioning aspects of our partnerships and our partners' failings that the core fantasies we have about love and relationships are revealed.

What love is not:

- It's not walking on eggshells. It's not being too nervous to share with our partners, to ask for things, to express our hurts or to challenge.
- It's not being superior. It's not thinking we know best.
- It's not making rude comments, being sarcastic, rolling our eyes, policing or correcting, making unfunny jokes or fault-finding.
- It's not bad-mouthing our partners to our friends. It's not laughing about them unkindly behind their backs, mocking them and ridiculing them.
- It's not complaining incessantly to anyone who will listen about our partners' failings.
- It's not relieving our partners of their responsibilities. It's not doing things for them or on their behalf. It's not enabling or rescuing.
- It's not feeling sorry for anyone; it's not feeling resentful.
- It's not withholding.
- It's not hiding behind a wall. It's not protecting ourselves at all costs.
- It's not great sex, or bad sex.
- It's not when we are scared of someone.
- It's not when we censor ourselves or play small.
- It's not dominating someone with our opinions, plans and preferences. It's not taking over.

- It's not giving someone scraps of attention and expecting that to be enough.
- It's not lying awake all night scared we're about to be rejected.
- It's not pretending relationships don't need work and that everything is fine.
- It's not blaming everything on our partners and having no insight into our own behaviour.
- It's not standing still.
- It's not saying I love you.
- It's not going through the motions.
- It's not wanting things to be different all the time.
- It's not staying quiet and not speaking up. It's not saying yes when we mean no.
- It's not sucking it up and tolerating bad behaviour.
- It's not wondering why we're lonely when our hearts are closed.
- It's not selfish and self-centred.

What love is:

- Not being hypervigilant to every detail, every mood, every opportunity to take something personally or exaggerate a negative intention.
- Going to our partners to share our thoughts and fears. Doing this from a place of trust and letting what they are able to give us be enough. Even if it's just a listening ear.
- Knowing our partners' hurts and recognising when they're being expressed or acted out.
- Choosing to believe in our partners. Encouraging them to fulfil their dreams and their potential without worrying or pointing out their flaws. We let them live their lives, making sure they know we are their biggest cheerleaders.

- Becoming masters of asking for help. 'Could you lend me a hand?', 'Would you mind helping me with this?', 'Let's do this together' become daily utterances. As do 'Thank you so much for your help', 'Your help means so much to me' and 'I love it when you do things with me.'
- Saying no if doing something is going to severely compromise our mental and emotional well-being. (This is not the same as putting ourselves out for our partners, which we need to do frequently. This means not automatically saying yes to things when it would be healthier for everyone involved if we said no.)
- Apologising. We are human and will make many errors and mistakes, knowingly or unknowingly. Apologising respects our partners and keeps pride and ego in check.
- Looking fondly at our partners. Admiring them, noticing their strengths, talents, things that are attractive and what makes them special – because they're there. They're always there. We just don't always see them.
- Knowing we're not perfect. We have insights into our flaws and can reflect on where we could have done better. This doesn't worsen our self-esteem; in fact, working on ourselves and being accountable improves it.
- Not allowing ourselves get too extreme in our thinking, behaving or communicating. All feelings are okay, but we are mindful not to let them escalate and become damaging. Emotional regulation, restraint, self-soothing, discipline and reining ourselves in are all things we do to maintain our self-respect and to respect the people we are with (which is covered in Chapter 7).

- Not insulting our partners. We may not like some of their actions, opinions or ideas, but we do not denigrate them with cruel and unkind language.
- Listening even if we don't agree (especially if we don't agree), even if it's hard to hear. We can ask that our partners keep it constructive and communicate with us in a respectful tone of voice and manner; however, it is our job to listen. Some of the most challenging conversations we will ever experience in our life will be in a romantic relationship. These can be profound and ultimately life-affirming. Pay attention.
- Prioritising teamwork. We see our partners as teammates and work together for a common goal because teams are stronger together.
- Allowing our partners be who they are. We can want things to change, improve and grow; however, we accept our partners. We don't become consumed with changing them and everything about them. We love them for who they are and we don't fall into the fault-finding trap.
- Tolerating difference. Sometimes our differences are extremely hard to come to terms with. We don't have to like them all but we can tolerate them.

That is secure love.

It's the absence of drama, it's the absence of panic and fear, it's the absence of games, and the absence of judgement and condemnation. It doesn't mean that there aren't ever problems, arguments, disagreements or hurt feelings. Secure attachments are still human attachments, but the key feature of securely attached relationships is *safety*.

We are safe to be who we are. We feel safe with the person we are with. And with that comes peace, trust and ease, the majority of the time.

When Ben got fired from his job, all he wanted to do was call his fiancée. In good times and bad, she was the first person he called. She knew him so well; he felt so cared for in the way she listened and commiserated. Just as when she'd had a health scare a few years ago, they had lots to figure out. It was scary and changes would need to be made, but they agreed 'they would get through it together'. They really supported each other and he was so grateful to have her in his life.

Secure Traits

These are some of the behavioural and emotional experiences that can occur when we are securely attached:

We are emotionally available

In the most simplified way, this is what secure attachment boils down to: we are emotionally available. We enjoy supporting other people and frequently allow others to support us too. There's an easy give and take to relationships that can only come about when we are not so guarded or isolated.

When we were growing up, we learnt about our emotions. The people in our environment were able to emotionally regulate themselves and help us manage our reactivity, which, over time, taught us to be able to regulate ourselves. This allowed us to mature emotionally and arrive in our adult lives with the skill of containment, with the tools to help us be robust and resilient in the face of life's inevitable challenges.

We can identify feelings and are happy to share them

with others. We don't expect others to fix or rescue us, but we trust our partners will respond to us. Due to this emotional availability, we are safe in our partnerships and our partners are safe with us.

We take our time getting to know people

We take our time getting to know someone, trusting them and falling in love with them. We are not mistrusting but we understand that trust is earned, not given. When meeting people, we take our time to learn about them, find out what's on offer with them and let them earn our trust. Falling in love is not a giant rollercoaster ride of emotions and premature intimacy, it is a gentle burn that will result in chemistry at the end, not necessarily the beginning.

We can read people quite well. Being in an emotionally regulated state, we can bring all our faculties when meeting people. We can observe other people's attitudes, their ways of dealing with things and their perspective on life. This gives us a pretty good read on who they are. We tune in to people's character, which is often where the locus of attraction lives for us.

We can talk about difficult stuff

We can have difficult conversations and believe in working through issues. Having self-worth, we know that difficult conversations are part of relationships and don't find them quite so daunting or frightening. We have sufficient self-esteem to know that when bad things happen it doesn't make us bad people. And generally, we like talking about things because a lack of communication or discussion is not what we are about. We accept that there will inevitably be many issues in our lives and relationships, and that these are to be worked through and often result in growth and further closeness.

We have self-esteem

Being secure means having a degree of self-esteem. We do not feel anxiety around relationships and we don't feel resistant to getting close to others or letting people in. We believe we are worthy of love.

Having self-esteem means holding ourselves in high regard. This is not grandiose; it doesn't mean we're superior. But it does mean we're going to recognise when people treat us poorly and not like it. It means we have the confidence to walk away from relationships that aren't right for us because we believe we deserve a certain level of commitment and interest.

When we have been raised being validated, valued and shown how to have self-esteem by people who possessed some themselves it is not hard for us to believe that people will like us and love us, and that partnership is something we can expect and enjoy.

Anxious and avoidant behaviours are ultimately about maintaining low self-esteem. **In our anxious attachment**, we are aware of our low self-esteem and feel bad about ourselves; **in our avoidance**, sometimes we are disconnected and, because of our grandiose defences, our low self-esteem lives hidden behind the scenes.

Becoming more secure changes all that.

Life is not an ongoing struggle

In our insecure attachment, life can feel like an endless grind. There's always something to be unhappy about and this can cause a lot of pain. Like any trauma, attachment trauma renders us alone in the world, soldiering on, often discouraged and dismayed, experiencing life and other people as one arduous, disheartening slog.

Being secure, we do not swing on a pendulum from one extreme to the other. We may have to live our lives without highs and lows, but our moderate, middle path offers us the ultimate accomplishment: stability. When we move out of survival mode and our nervous systems are calm the vast majority of the time, we have arrived at security.

Being stable and emotionally regulated, we do not experience feelings as overwhelming, and there is a natural buffer in place to make sure we do not become too extreme in our thinking and emoting. We find we don't really like emotional rollercoaster rides, and definitely not in our relationships.

We are open and flexible (and have easy limits)

Imagine not always needing to be defensive. Imagine going through life in a trusting way, not having a heart that's closed, not being dogmatic and dominating, or passive and people-pleasing. When we are more secure it is not difficult for us to be easy-going because we value relationships and community; we like to fit in with the group so it's not a big deal to be agreeable. However, we have an inbuilt sense when we can no longer be flexible. We know our limits. We don't steamroller over our own boundaries and we don't try to be everything to everyone. We are ourselves and that feels enough.

We tolerate (not extreme) lack of proximity

Enjoying a romantic moment with your partner? And then needing to say goodbye to them as they leave for work? We might feel a bit sad but we can do it; we adapt easily from being with our partners to being on our own. A huge part of secure attachment is trusting in our connection with our partners, regardless of their presence.

Our secure base becomes the starting point for us to go out into the world and achieve our goals and chase our dreams. We often have independent lives to our partners, and our base – the relationship – is our stabiliser. We don't need to be around each other all the time, but we really enjoy it when we are.

We encourage ourselves and our partners to lead big lives, to stretch themselves to do and be all they wish to. This is a great indicator of love indeed.

Deep down, we all crave love and acceptance. This is part of being human and is a great joy of our life experience. Uncovering our attachment tendencies can be overwhelming. There is a lot that goes on in our relationships – each of us is complicated and distinct with so much of what has been described so far. This is why many of us find relationships hard. Learning relationship skills, understanding how love is demonstrated, and replacing fear with courage and compassion is what will move us away from our insecure leanings to the more enriching and peaceful contentment of secure partnerships. This is the focus for Part III.

Journalling prompts

- Which aspects of 'what love is not' have you experienced? Describe.
- Which aspects of 'what love is' have you experienced? Describe.
- Which aspects from both lists and this chapter do you need to work on?
- Can you think of relationships, or times in your relationships, when you felt most secure? What created the safety for you?
- What feelings came up as you read this chapter? Reflect on why.

Solutions: Breaking the Pattern

Our immediate reactions and responses are often not our best. They are unlikely to be the ones that will help us to achieve our goals. They are based on assumptions, fears and our stories, and keep us unconsciously repeating the very patterns we are trying to break. This section is about learning skills and tools to help us observe our knee-jerk instincts, pause, and bring more intentional thought to how we might respond in different ways.

In order for things to improve, we need to focus our energy and efforts on making small, significant changes. We can keep on responding the same way and get the same results, or we can do something different and create a new possibility.

CHAPTER 6

It Starts With You

To overcome our insecure ways, we need to look at ourselves. We need to develop our relational intelligence as well as our emotional intelligence. This will help us to accept difficult truths, such as the many grey areas that exist within human dynamics, how subjective our interpretations are, how much of a negative bias we have when it comes to matters of the heart, and how defensive we can be when feeling vulnerable.

This chapter explores the starting point of the work. It encourages you to examine your mindset and root out resistance, fear, defensiveness and behaviour or thinking that will block growth. We do the work when we're ready, and this chapter gets you ready.

The Behaviours Holding Us Back

Living in denial

Rather than living life, we cope with life, and one of the most effective ways of coping with life is trying to be one step removed from ourselves at all times.

Denial plays a big part in our survival. This is illustrated by how many people don't like going to the doctor or asking for help. In order to keep going, it seems to be best to deny the more concerning aspects of our human frailty.

Our work is about slowly and consistently challenging our denial. This is when it's useful to remember that we are not aware of the vast majority of our thoughts and behaviours as they are completely unconscious. We can be laser-focused on our partners and their less-than-ideal contributions to the relationship, but must concede we can lack precious little insight into our own. Denial blocks responsibility, empathy and growth.

Beneath our denial, deep down, we all know there are things we're not facing up to, some responsibility we are dodging or pain we are trying to outrun. And our world is designed to help us do that. We have every opportunity to distract and divert ourselves from the present moment and our uncomfortable reality.

Having read the previous chapters, you will have gone some way to challenging a lot of your denial. Are you aware of minimising your problems? Of struggling to be accountable for getting your needs met and experiencing happiness? We are people on the run. We are running from ourselves – and many of us have lost our way.

Acting defensively, aka hiding our sensitivity

I have never met anyone who did not respond with sensitivity to the pain and difficulty of relationships. We are all extremely sensitive. Even if it's hidden behind resentment, accusations, sadness, criticism, stonewalling, anger, complaining, crying – we are sensitive. We impact each other. I cannot overstate how important this is. *What we do to each other matters.* We exert huge power over one another but we seldom take responsibility for this. The very first step in more relational ways of being is understanding that you are a sensitive human being and you are in a relationship with another sensitive human being.

There is only one way to move out of defensiveness with each other and that is to stop giving each other reasons to be defensive. Yes, bad things may have happened. Terrible things have probably been said. Feelings have been hugely hurt. You might both be wounded. So let's stop wounding each other, right now. Let's stop trying to communicate indirectly to get a reaction from our partners. Let's stop withdrawing and let's stop contorting ourselves to whatever we think our partners need us to be. We can start what will probably be a lifelong pursuit: being ourselves and letting our partners be who they are, too.

Being judgemental

Being judged by the people we love does not feel great. It's easy to sneer and scorn, to make snap conclusions based on not very much information. It's much more challenging to be non-judgemental, as this requires an acceptance of others that few of us have. We are becoming more and more intolerant, and we are quick to judge others as good or bad, right or wrong (with ourselves usually occupying the good and right categories, of course). We point out our partners' problematic traits and behaviour, judging them for every little thing they do. Then we are surprised when our love wanes and desire decreases.

Being judgemental blocks love and care. Tenderness cannot exist with its harshness. It's a way of creating distance between ourselves and our loves, which isn't what we're aiming for in our intimate lives.

How different things would be if we could just be less judgemental.

Over- or under-responsibility

What is your instinctive response when someone you like wants something from you? Do you feel excited and flattered? Nervous and giddy? Or alarmed and overwhelmed?

Our relationship with responsibility reveals our attachment wounding, and the associations we have when it comes to being there for other people. Some people have had to be responsible from a very young age. They assume the role of responsibility within the family and this generally stays with them for life. They naturally take the lead in certain matters and can take responsibility even when it's not wanted or required.

Other people resist responsibility at all costs. Responsibility feels like demands on the self that are just too high. For some people, taking other people into account, being leaned on and being needed feels like a prison.

Again, these two positions are about occupying extremes. Our aim, however, is to be neither over-responsible nor under-responsible.

Learning appropriate responsibility can be a tough road for people with either anxious or avoidant attachment, as both positions show the person's unhealthily safe place. Over-responsible people have a perceived sense of control and under-responsible people have a perceived sense of freedom. Over-responsible people will settle for being needed rather than being loved, and under-responsible people will settle for isolation and quiet rather than emotional messiness. Neither are allowing themselves to be loved for who they are and neither are experiencing a fundamental human need: to be cared for.

By caring for everyone else or not caring for anyone at all we rob ourselves of the true and equal partnerships that are possible. When do we get to be held, looked after or cherished? If we don't change our way of doing things, the answer might be never.

How to Be More Relational

Part of learning to develop and mature out of insecure attachment to more secure bonds is about learning how to be more relational. Being relational means focusing on and valuing the 'us' of a relationship more than the 'I' of ourselves/the individual. When we are relationally intelligent, we are able to appreciate that relationships are fundamental to the human experience. We believe that they contribute to a fulfilling life and our emotional well-being. We take responsibility for our impact on others and allow others to impact us.

We can develop our relational skills by learning to fully contribute to and participate in our relationships, share our thoughts and feelings with each other, negotiate, set boundaries, and develop a way of being in a relationship that benefits the relationship. That is my aim with this book. I want you to reflect on your behaviour to see if it is beneficial to your relationships. We can strive to be accountable for our actions and take responsibility for whatever is taking place – both good and not-so-good.

Learning how to be relational means enlarging our perspectives and our scope to include not just our own needs but our partners', equally. This means we take someone else into account, consider their feelings and behave lovingly towards them. However, in the unhappy landscape of a struggling relationship, this can be very challenging indeed.

Before we focus on developing more specific relational skills in the chapters that follow, let's first discuss what we need in order to do the work.

Having insight into your own behaviour

If we want things to improve in our relationships, we have to take responsibility for the thought processes and behaviours that are getting in our way. And in order to do that we need to know ourselves pretty well. So much of our behaviour is unconscious, which means a lot of the time we don't know what we are doing or why we are doing it. It's going to take great honesty, and a dollop of humility, for us to learn about ourselves and commit to changing the behaviours that are not serving us. We need to take our forensic eye off our partners and loved ones, and instead place it firmly on ourselves.

It is extremely tempting to simply explain away relational difficulties due to the personality and circumstances of the people with whom we are having the difficulty. Indeed, this is what the vast majority of people do. We shrug our shoulders, pointing the finger at them, and go about our lives without taking (genuine) responsibility for anything. It is very difficult to grow if this is our attitude. Perhaps the lion's share of the blame *is* to be put at your partner's feet. But even if that is the case, how does that help us develop within ourselves? We must learn to reflect on the only person's behaviour that we can change: our own.

We cannot control other people; we can only control ourselves. With that in mind, we need to face up to the parts of us that might need a little bit more love, a gentle prod, a lot more responsibility or a total rethink. This is not so bad. In fact, it's incredibly liberating. Once we start doing this, we can become eager to hear feedback and enjoy being challenged, because being fully awake to ourselves means anything is possible, which is pretty damn exhilarating.

Grace did not realise what a dominating person she was. She had opinions, sure – didn't everyone, though? She was comfortable with 'animated' disagreements and harsh arguments, her body language as loud as her voice, her language ferocious and sometimes cutting. After conflict, she would carry on with her life while her partner struggled to comprehend what had just happened; they would think, 'Is the relationship over? Does Grace hate me?' while she would just shrug it off and move on.

It took a while for Grace to realise that what felt natural for her felt jarring for her partner. That her 'letting off steam' had ramifications for her partner, like feeling hurt, disrespected and put down. She lacked insight into her own behaviour and the impact it could sometimes have on others.

By remembering her fights with her sister growing up, how nasty they could get and how torn apart Grace would feel afterwards, she realised she was putting her partner in the same harrowing position. This was a lightbulb moment for her and the beginning of her taking responsibility for how she automatically and unthinkingly vented, and the highly negative effect that was having on her relationship.

Willingness to change and grow

We can't move forward in any meaningful way unless we have a willingness to do so. Some individuals are fortunate enough to have a strong drive to work, grow, do better and keep learning. Other individuals struggle to understand the need for change and lack motivation to do so. As you read this book, you can assess your own willingness to do things differently, to help yourself create a happier future.

Change is not easy for humans. We have brains designed to automate our responses, that like predictability and routine. Change, as an idea, is very appealing; however, even if we know what we need to do differently - and that in itself is pretty rare - changing, and maintaining change, is hard. Anyone who has made New Year's resolutions knows just how difficult it is to implement change and then keep it going. When we have entrenched ways of doing things, often years if not decades old, we will slowly or quickly shift back to those ways before we know it.

That's why it is so much better to focus on growth rather than change.

If we can stretch ourselves a little bit, we push ourselves in ways that will help us. Being a bit more patient, for example, is a worthwhile pursuit. We may not be able to completely change our temperament but we can commit ourselves to being more patient, which will help us manage our negative reactions and slowly create new behaviours. We don't so much change who and what we are, but we begin to take responsibility for our current circumstances and make positive adaptations to help us grow in ways that will increase our relational skills.

If there's anything that will help you fulfil your dreams, it's willingness. If nothing else at all, we can work on always being willing. Without it, all is lost.

Ensuring safety

Our work is always about creating safety, because when we are unsafe we immediately become insecure, as our nervous system gets triggered (see page 65). Maintaining a regulated nervous system is what allows us to relate in the most calm, caring and compassionate way. When we are unsafe we have to go into protective mode, and all our natural defences and fears come to the fore.

Creating safety is what will heal our attachment trauma and also allow us to take responsibility for ourselves and our relationships. So many of our behaviours maintain the lack of safety in our lives. We can challenge ourselves: what is it that maintains an activated nervous system? Things like working too late, too long or overworking in general; rushing and walking too fast; not taking care of ourselves and over-functioning; saying unsupportive statements to ourselves; gossiping and involving ourselves with drama; engaging with people who are not good for our mental health; too much drinking and drugging; not getting enough sleep and having a poor diet are examples most of us can relate to.

We want to be safe people ourselves. If we are critical of ourselves or others, if we are constantly hard on ourselves and others, we are unsafe. Our nervous systems will be activated. As humans, we can only relax when someone is in charge and we know they have our best interests at heart. *We need to be that someone.*

In relationships, we can work at being respectful, maintaining peacefulness, talking things out rather than shouting things out, being constructive, and being helpful rather than unhelpful. All of this creates a safe, secure partnership. This must be our goal.

Even when we're arguing, we should still be safe. No one is going to get too dysregulated, impulsively end the relationship or character assassinate the other person.

It's a useful idea to keep coming back to: what does emotional safety look like here? Is what I am doing safe for me and safe for my partner? How can we make things feel safer? Does this atmosphere feel safe? Is my effort going into creating safety or creating conflict?

In this way, no one is right and no one is wrong; no one is put in their place or punished. No one is given the cold shoulder. None of that matters. What matters is that we are safe, solid and secure.

Increasing cooperation and agreeableness

There is so much denial around this one! And often so much pushback. For some of us, cooperating with our partners feels like a huge weakness. In fact, many of us make sure we don't cooperate with our partners. We are actively obstructive. Even in everyday interactions, we are combative, sarcastic and unhelpful.

Why are we so intent on getting in the way of harmony? Why does agreeableness and cooperation feel like we are losing and our partners are winning? And when did relationships become a place where there are winners and losers?

As we've seen, secure attachment means we are a team. We are working for the greater good. We love and support each other, and the last people on earth we need to fight are our partners. Relationships are where we go for peace – they're not a battleground. Being a fighter is wonderful – we are strong, we don't give up, we are determined – but it also means that we can easily tip over into survival mode. Without a sense of safety, we will need to be protective of ourselves, suspicious of others and not giving an inch.

As we will explore in the upcoming chapters, we would do well to focus all our efforts away from defending ourselves and keeping people at arm's length and towards improving the associations we have about other people and relationships. In unlearning the need to be alone, and to be on the attack, we can instead learn the deep contentment of being part of something bigger than ourselves: a relationship, a family, with everyone working together for the well-being of all. This is what we're fighting for. We need to fight the part of ourselves that won't let people in.

But we also need to not tolerate bad behaviour

There are those of us who are overly accommodating, who are nervous to speak up and don't want to upset the applecart. Sometimes, bad behaviour and unhealthy dynamics have become normalised and we are too passive in our relationships and our lives. We can feel exhausted by our partners or the adversity in our relationships, and we have long since ceased to spend time thinking about whether someone or something is right for us. This is also when we can blame ourselves for all the ills in the relationship, internalising our pain or turning our anger on ourselves. We accept half-lives and empty relationships; we withdraw into ourselves or we act out in various coping activities, like food, work, drink or exercise.

Do you feel you are growing in yourself and your relationship? Are you having the relationship you want or are you having the relationship your partner wants? Did you give up somewhere along the line and are now just going through the motions? It's all too common to stagnate in our partnerships and lose sight of our happiness and real connection with our partners. When was the last time you made a request in your relationship? When you said no instead of yes? Or when you felt important and valued? If these are missing, there's work to do.

Being secure is about being awake and alive in our

relationships. To *have relationships*. Many people merely exist together, where the partnership, marriage or relationship is very hollow indeed.

We need to see the reality of our relationships, work on them, put effort in, stand up for ourselves and see if a future with our partners can be any different.

Learnt helplessness

- Do you feel unhappily stuck in your life or relationship?
- Do you not know what to do to make things better?
- Do you feel 'it is what it is' and there's nothing to be done?
- Are you constantly waiting for your life to improve?
- Do you feel angry, upset or bitter about how endlessly difficult life is?
- Do things always go wrong for you?
- Do you cry or complain all the time about how awful your life is?

Learnt helplessness is when we have been taught we have no power in our own lives. We may have had an upbringing that was quite out of control, with dysfunctional home environments or parents/caregivers who had unhealthy relationships, addiction issues or mental health conditions that were frightening. We learnt that life and people are terrifying and there's nothing we can do about it. This programmed us to not have agency in our own lives, a belief system we take with us into our adulthood. If no one supported us or looked after us we learnt to do the same: we don't support ourselves or look after ourselves. We don't do anything. We've learnt to be helpless.

Our work now is to challenge the entrenched idea that we don't have power in our lives to bring about change. The following chapters will show you how to take back appropriate power, be proactive, make esteeming choices for yourself, and approach your life with a sense of confidence and capability.

Respecting self and others

Sometimes, this can be a bit of a hidden process but it is a significant one. Consider your life and the people who you deeply respect – there might be people you admire, look up to, aspire to be like or just appreciate having in your life. Some of us can think of lots of people we respect. In many ways, we respect everyone. But some of us might struggle to think of *anyone* we respect. Who really deserves our respect anyway? If we've experienced serious hurt we don't grow up feeling respected and we therefore don't respect others. People have proven to be quite a let-down.

This is important for our relationships because respect underscores everything that takes place in a healthy, secure partnership. Our partners might behave in ways that frustrate and annoy us, of course, but ultimately, it's healthy and appropriate to hold those we love in high regard.

Respecting someone does not mean condoning behaviour or agreeing with them all the time; it simply means, on a very basic, human level, we can treat them with civility and politeness. Redefining what respect means in this way can be helpful. We are not being submissive to anyone but being a respectful human in the world. In our relationships, however, if we cannot respect our partners and treat them with respect the vast majority of the time, this is definitely something to work on. We'll delve further into this and explore the tools that will help in Chapter 9.

It is not our partners' job to earn our respect or behave in ways that demand it. If we claim to love someone, that means we respect them. We will speak respectfully. We will not put them down, hurt them on purpose or look down on them. That's on us.

The Importance of Self-Care

I have sat with so many clients over the years who have grappled with pain and difficulty in their relationships. There is a saying in therapy that sometimes the people in therapy are there because of the people in their life who won't go to therapy. Our partners, family or loved ones may be workaholic, anxious, avoidant, have anger issues, have financial problems or struggle with mental health issues, and the stress of dealing with that can weigh heavily on *our* shoulders. We can desperately want things to improve but as we can't change other people, little seems to get better. In fact, the only change that seems to take place is a negative one within us.

We neglect ourselves and our own needs and our health suffers as a result. We can burn out, we can get depressed, we can feel anxious, we can have sleep problems, we don't eat properly, we drink or drug too much and we can lose ourselves entirely. And because our partners have so many of their own issues, and we are so focused on those, our struggles can go unacknowledged.

Like much behaviour, how we care for ourselves and look after ourselves is a learnt behaviour. For those of us with an insecure attachment style, the way we have been taught to look after ourselves does not always meet our real needs. Some of us believe that self-care is about bubble baths, treats and spoiling ourselves, but true self-care is about learning to meet our needs, taking responsibility for ourselves and making sure our well-being is always a priority.

Looking after ourselves in relationships is particularly crucial. If we are hungry for love and crave acceptance, sometimes we can lose our voice in our relationships, not wanting to upset our partners and cause any problems. We can be hesitant and hold ourselves back when it comes to stating our needs (sometimes not even knowing what those needs are). Likewise, if we were brought up in an aggressive or a passive-aggressive household, we've learnt to get our needs met through shouting or conflict or indirect behaviours.

Self-care in the context of relationships is learning to look after ourselves, validating our own needs and doing our best to meet those needs, and asking our partners to meet those needs too. Because it is *self*-care, however, the vast amount is done by ourselves. We need to have our own back, knowing we will look after ourselves and trusting we can get ourselves through anything.

Self-care means putting down boundaries, it means going to the doctor when we're not well, it means developing relational skills so we can have equal and loving relationships, it's taking regular breaks and time away from work to replenish, it's learning about ourselves and it's keeping ourselves happy and healthy. This is our job. This is self-care.

Self-responsibility is not the same as selfishness.

Note: sometimes people can corrupt self-care, calling it selfish. It is absolutely imperative that we learn to be accountable in our own lives and responsible for ourselves. And we do this through self-care. We don't expect to be rescued and we don't deny our own needs; we understand that caring for ourselves is important and we make sure that we do it. If we go into some sort of guilt process or feel it is self-indulgent, we do not understand what self-care is. Looking after ourselves is a starting point to being adult. We are responsible for ourselves, we take good care of ourselves and, as a result, we are able to interact with others in healthy and esteeming ways. We don't accept bad behaviour, we don't turn a blind eye to things that are hurtful to us, and we do the difficult work of standing up for ourselves when required.

Many of us want better relationships but don't know where to start. There are mechanics to how a partnership can function at its best and, if we get those mechanics right, we can use them to tackle whatever lies ahead for us. Without them, we can fall at the first, most basic hurdles. This chapter has outlined the attitudes and behaviours we can nurture in ourselves that set us up for success. In the next chapters, we will learn the skills and tools we need for our relationships to flourish and thrive.

Journalling prompts

- Are you aware of the behaviours that are holding you back? Do you have insight into your own behaviour and what you need to work on? Make a note of what feels pertinent to you:
  - Being defensive: closed off, quick to react and blame, deflect, collapse into tears/despair
  - Being judgemental: labelling good or bad, condemning, assuming the one-up (superior) or one-down (inferior) position, needing to be right

- ° Over- or under-responsible: rescuing others or wanting to be rescued, taking over, doing the bare minimum, knowing best or learnt helplessness
- Think of previous relationships or moments in your partnerships and consider how emotionally safe or unsafe they were. Give examples.
- What do you regret tolerating in your history and do not wish to repeat in the future?
- In what ways could you respect yourself and others more? (We'll cover this in Chapter 9.)
- What elements of self-care will help support you doing this work and building your resilience?

CHAPTER 7

Emotional Regulation

Feelings are so convincing. When we are feeling big stuff in our relationship those feelings can quickly take over and they begin controlling us. If we feel angry, we can lash out and hurt others or ourselves. When we feel jealous, we react by being suspicious and hypervigilant. When we feel disregarded, our self-esteem plummets. Emotions dictate our behaviour and then our behaviour can become highly self-defeating. When we are emotionally dysregulated we are out of control, but often we are so awash with our emotions, *we don't care*. This is when we behave in ways that we either later regret or thereafter need to defend to the death, which only worsens the situation.

One of the most important skills we can learn is the ability to emotionally regulate. As we learnt on page 65, our nervous systems get activated frequently and it is crucial we return ourselves to a sense of stability and calm, so we are not repeatedly keeping the nervous system on high alert. As we've explored, to be securely attached is when the body feels safe, even during relationship difficulty. The first – most important – step towards being more secure is not letting our emotions rule us. We need to recognise when we've lost control and commit ourselves to learning how to manage our emotions so we are safe, our partners are safe and our relationships are safe.

When we were growing up, very few of us were taught the art of self-soothing or recognising our emotions. In our adult lives now, we need to begin validating and understanding them, self-soothing and using our emotions to enrich our lives and inform our decisions.

Tolerating difficult emotions is key to relational resilience. Emotional regulation is not about pushing down our feelings, sucking it up, condoning bad behaviour or pretending everything is okay when it's not. Emotional regulation is about taking responsibility for thoughts and actions that are not in keeping with our values or likely to fulfil our goals.

Sometimes, I can see when clients have been emotionally dysregulated in an extreme way for a very long time. They are unable to sit still or relax completely. Their nervous system is continuously activated, ominously ticking over, an alarm always ready – and about – to go off.

We can use emotional regulation skills on a daily basis – when we know we're going to have a difficult conversation or when we find ourselves in the middle of a difficult conversation and emotions are running high.

Signs you are dysregulated

Sometimes it's very obvious when we are dysregulated: our heart is racing; our body is shaking; we are anxious, frightened or annoyed; we feel agitated and overwhelmed, and our anger is overflowing. Or, conversely, we can feel ourselves completely shut off; the shutters come down and we will check out. We get fed up, overwhelmed or just too jaded to be present and engaged in the relationship, so we push our partners away. We can do this by being rude or dismissive, repelling our partners by picking a fight, or doing or saying something insensitive.

It can also be quite subtle and come out in our ways of behaving and thinking. We are cynical and sarcastic, or people-pleasing and passive. We aren't sleeping well, we have digestive problems and we are unable to relax. All these examples show how powerfully our emotions can impact our lives.

The Window of Tolerance

As the name suggests, the window of tolerance speaks about the optimum zone we are in when we are able to tolerate emotions and reactions, and we are at our most human. We can have empathy, be kind, think and respond constructively, and not be activated into either extreme of fight or freeze.

From a relational point of view, this is incredibly important. When insecurely attached, we are easily activated and leave the window of tolerance, going into hyperarousal, where we are quick to react into fight mode, escalating conflict and exacerbating problems, or we can react into hypoarousal, where we shut down, zone out and go into freeze.

This is where emotional regulation comes in. In order to maintain our mental and emotional health, we need to be able to ride the waves of our emotions rather than be thrown around on an emotional rollercoaster. Emotional regulation skills allow us to keep our systems deactivated, increase our ability to tolerate distress and difficulty, and stay on an even keel.

When we are avoidantly attached, emotionally regulating often helps us bring ourselves *back* to our emotions and reality. When we are anxiously attached, emotional regulation means calming down enough to access our deeper emotions and reality.

How to self-soothe

Self-soothing helps us not to be reactive or explosive/implosive. It helps us to take control of our behaviour so we can begin doing things differently, more in keeping with our values and goals.

- **Be a comfort to yourself:** What we often do instead is rile ourselves up. We are hurting and we can make ourselves hurt even more – listening to sad music, telling our friends about all the negatives over and over. We need to soothe those hurt feelings with compassion and comfort.
- **Reduce the upset:** We can be at the mercy of our triggered emotions. We catastrophise the future, demonise our partners, feel hopeless and despairing – and we believe it all. Feelings are not facts and we need to recognise thoughts and feelings to be transient and ever-changing.
- **Be true to yourself:** Who do you want to be? And what do you need to do to be that person? We can lose our value system and moral code in relationships so it's important to stay connected to who we are. Soothing yourself with a clear idea of who you want to be can guide you in your behaviours and choices.

- **Give yourself the gift of time:** Our reactions are often top-level emotions and we don't get to what lives several layers down, which are our fears, needs, wishes and dreams. Those are far more meaningful than our defensive retaliations. You can give yourself time to calm down and get in touch with what really matters.
- **Restore resilience:** We all want to be emotionally robust. That means developing the skill of tolerating life's challenges and difficulties without dysregulating or acting out. If we are easily reactive we are not especially robust. We are often in survival mode and defensive much of the time.

Learning to withstand the discomfort of emotional difficulty is very challenging. However, we can develop higher tolerance and become more resilient. This is the reward for self-soothing – we can manage ourselves and our emotions and behave with dignity and composure.

Emotional Regulation Skills and Techniques

Many of the skills in this chapter come from dialectical behaviour therapy (DBT), pioneered by Dr Marsha Linehan. This form of therapy is highly practical and is based on the premise that we can seize control of all our thoughts and behaviour and create a happy, meaningful life. It is a therapy that validates our emotions and experiences, helps us to conceptualise what we do based on our childhood and upbringing (which often was invalidating), and helps us to adapt our thinking and behaviour to be more constructive. It provides superb skills and tools to help us manage our emotions, so we can have healthier interpersonal relationships and lives.

Learn to STOP

This is arguably the single most important regulation skill we can learn. The power of pausing, stopping, apprehending ourselves, learning to stop is a sign of emotional maturity and staying in control of ourselves.

How it works:

S: STOP

Stop doing whatever you're doing. Stop saying whatever you're saying. When you notice you are losing control and your emotions are in charge, either escalating conflict or numbing out, you need to stop. Pause. This helps you not to do any further damage and gives you a moment to change your trajectory. Try to think about the emotions you're experiencing and put a label on them.

T: TAKE A STEP BACK

When we are over- or under-emotional we are overwhelmed. Too much is happening and we need to take a step back, take a deep breath and get a better understanding of the situation. We may need to do some breathing exercises, mindfulness or grounding techniques that we know work for us (see page 173 for some easy breathing exercises). This step allows you to get back in control of what you are doing and saying.

O: OBSERVE

As you focus on your breathing and reflect on your situation, you can observe what is happening around and within you. You can notice your automatic negative thoughts (ANTs – see opposite) and remind yourself of how unconscious and rooted in fear-based beliefs they are. You can be aware of catastrophising or jumping to conclusions. In this step, you can look at the relevant facts available rather than just your emotions and feelings. Chapter 8 goes into much more detail about distorted thinking.

P: PROCEED MINDFULLY

At this point, you can ask yourself what you want from your current situation. And you can remind yourself that you have the choice now to make things better or to make things worse. Once you have arrived at this step, you should be calmer and you should certainly be in control. This allows you to think things through and be mindful about what you are going to do next. As you proceed, do so cautiously and with resolution and constructiveness as your guide.

If you are avoidantly attached, you need to be careful that stopping is not the same as shutting down. Ideally, you want to stop the shutting down. An added element for you could be remembering the good in your partner: remind yourselves of what you like about them, what you are fond of, what you find attractive, admirable and sexy. When we shut down, we shut down to the people in our life and we can begin a devaluing process. We need to stay in the reality of our partners, reminding ourselves of all the good and amazing aspects to them. This, again, will help you to proceed mindfully in a way that is true to you and also respectful of your partner.

If you are anxiously attached, stopping gives you a great opportunity not to go on an emotional rollercoaster ride. You can remind yourself to stay in control at all times and not let your emotions run the show. Also remember, however, that stopping does not mean that you negate your emotions or dismiss them. Rather, as you observe what is going on, you can access what your emotions are trying to tell you. Sometimes our reactivity can hijack what we're thinking and feeling, sending us down the wrong roads. By taking a step back, breathing and observing what is going on for you, you can access what's really important and what you would like to share or discuss.

Don't let the ANTs bite you

We all have automatic negative thoughts (ANTs). They can often be quite random in nature or they can be specific to ourselves and our circumstances. We aren't consciously aware of our ANTs - they just happen. This is an unconscious process and is often where a lot of negative bias can live. In the extreme, ANTs can be a contributing factor to depression and anxiety. This is another example of how our brains are not on our side (see page 69). Our lives are very different in our modern society - we are not under serious threat all day, every day. However, the protective part of our brain still believes we are.

In order to survive, we are wired to notice the negative. From a relational standpoint, this is deeply unhelpful and we need to be very effortful in challenging and noticing our ANTs. Because ANTs can bite you.

Helicopter view

This is a brilliant skill because it reminds us of the bigger picture. Sometimes, when we are in distress, upset or annoyed, we can over-focus on minute details that are not particularly relevant to our relationship as a whole. We can trip over the small obstacles unnecessarily. Taking a helicopter view invites us to zoom out and look at the bigger picture.

Ask yourself the following questions to help you gain perspective:

- What would the situation look like to someone watching who isn't emotionally involved?
- What am I reacting to? What does the situation mean to me?
- What is the best thing to do next? For me, the other person and the situation?

If you are avoidantly attached, helicopter view is helpful because it allows you to think of action. In your avoidance, you can take a step back from the relationship, preferring to do nothing or withdraw. Because the final question invites you to consider the next right thing to do, you can challenge yourself to think of a positive action that will enhance your relationship, rather than create further ill feeling. This is not a pressure, however, because you can do it in a way that feels comfortable for you. We can be ever reminded to 'avoid avoidance' and to stay connected to our partners in ways that don't feel too compromising. Remember, the question is what is the best thing to do for yourself and the other person. This is a great learning opportunity to be more relational.

If you are anxiously attached, this is a useful skill as it helps you question what is going on for you, but also helps to reinforce the skill you need to learn, which is more objectivity at times. When you think how this might look to someone who is not emotionally involved, it can give you an impartial view, free from your fears and worries, allowing you to be more grounded. You are also challenged practically about what you want to do next. Sometimes our emotions can take us over and we are more interested in venting than thinking about problem-solving and moving forward.

Change, accept or let go

When you feel really stuck in your relationship or in an interaction with your partner, you can remind yourself of your options. Often, we want to take responsibility for our partners and change them in some way, or we want to be under-responsible and passive and not do anything at all. The truth of the matter, however, is that there are few options when it comes to life or relationships.

This DBT skill suggests we have three options:

1. **We can change.**
   For example: We can do everything we can to change the relationship in ways that we would like. We can change our own reactions and attitudes to alter our experience of the relationship, and that in turn will change the dynamic. This represents a lot of the work we are doing in this book. We are looking at our own behaviour and seeing how we can change in ways to bring about more security in our lives and relationships. When we make changes, we change the nature of our relationships, and often our relationships change too. However, we have no control over other people and cannot change them.

2. **We can accept.**
   For example: We can ask ourselves: 'Can I accept things as they are? If nothing were to change in my

relationship, would I still want to be in it? Can I accept my partner?' We can strive to accept our partners for who they are and not be so focused on changing them in significant ways. Acceptance is a demonstration of love and that can be part of our work. If we cannot accept the way things are, and we've done everything we can to change, then we are left with the final option . . .

3. We can let go.

For example: If there is change that needs to happen and it has not, and we cannot accept the status quo, we have no other choice than to let go. Perhaps you feel you have put everything you can into your relationship and have nothing left to give. Perhaps you have tried to accept your partner as they are, wholeheartedly loving them, non-judgementally and with kindness, and yet you are unable to progress. If that is the case, your only other option is to let go. We cannot be in a loving relationship when we are fundamentally not accepting of the person we claim to love. We must know ourselves well enough to recognise when we are not accepting someone as they are. If our partners are not going to change in the way we need, it is therefore right for us to let this relationship go.

If you are avoidantly attached, sometimes you can jump to the letting go part of this tool. You don't challenge yourself to grow and change, and you certainly don't try to accept your partner as they are. You can be a bit reckless and leave the relationship too soon, without really trying to stretch yourself and widen your understanding of love and care.

If you are anxiously attached, you can get stuck in the change part of the skill. You can become fixated on the change you want to see in your partner or changing yourself in every conceivable way, which is not healthy. You also need to practise acceptance – allowing your partner to be who they are and seeing if that can be enough. Likewise, letting go can be hard. You stay hanging on, despite feeling bitterly unhappy and unable to accept your partner as they are, making the relationship an endless project. This is not esteeming or appropriate and can create ill-feeling in the relationship. Spending more time on acceptance or considering letting go is a good stretch for you. Acceptance allows us to see what is genuinely on offer from our partners; letting go shows us what we can do when what is on offer is not right for us.

Breathwork

Breathing can be a quick way to calm down and de-escalate ourselves or it can be a daily practice that helps us to stay regulated and grounded as we go about our lives. It's wonderful if we can incorporate breathwork into our lives for both benefits, as it will set us up to create the best chance of success in our lives and in our relationships.

4-7-8 BREATHING

This breathing exercise can be used to reduce anxiety. For example, during a difficult conversation, before an important meeting or to help you fall asleep. Breathe in for four seconds, hold your breath for seven seconds and breathe out for eight seconds. Repeat this four times, twice a day.

BOX BREATHING

This exercise is also known as 'four-square breathing' and is favoured by the Navy SEALs to prepare for high-pressure situations. Exhale for four seconds, then pause for four seconds, inhale for four seconds, and hold your breath for four seconds. Repeat this four times, several times a day as needed.

Body scan

The purpose of the body scan is to become more conscious of our body and tune in to our feelings and sensations. It can help our ability to focus and be present as it teaches us to be more aware of what we're experiencing in the here and now.

First get comfortable, then begin to breathe deeply, closing your eyes. From the top of your head, mentally scan down your body. Take your time. Notice how you feel physically, where there is tension or relaxation, tightness or flexibility. Without judgement, bring your attention and your breath to your body, not trying to change anything, simply noticing. Do this on every part of your body, finishing at your feet and toes. It can take as long as you would like/are able and can be repeated multiple times a day.

Co-Regulation

While regulating our emotions is ultimately our own responsibility, and the vast majority of the time we are required to do it on our own, learning to co-regulate can be a very bonding and healing experience for people in relationships. It can be a huge demonstration of love and care to our partners, and will help in times of anxious or avoidant ways of relating when the nervous system is activated.

Co-regulating is when we allow someone to help us to regulate, so it's very important that the other person isn't dysregulated! We are allowing someone else's calm nervous system to reassure and calm our nervous system. This can be through physical holding or touch, like hand-holding, or simply a person's incredibly affirming physical presence.

What happens in many relationships is one or more people become dysregulated and then everyone involved gets activated, often escalating any conflict or difficulty. By understanding the importance of emotional regulation, we can keep ourselves regulated and if we notice someone we love becoming dysregulated, help them and their nervous system to deactivate. So rather than worsening the conflict, throwing more fuel on the fire, name-calling or otherwise making things worse, we instead choose to be extremely loving and compassionate, and reduce the conflict and the difficulty.

Ways to co-regulate

Physical touch:

- embrace, standing, sitting or lying down
- rubbing or massaging back
- heart hug breathing (see page 177)
- hand-holding
- comforting physical presence

Calming and comforting words, for example:

- 'I can understand you are upset.'
- 'We are going to figure this out.'
- 'I am listening.'
- 'Everything is going to be okay.'
- 'Nothing bad is going to happen.'
- 'I love you.'

Meeting your partner's needs:
  Ask your partner what it is they need in this moment. This might be reassurance and affection, a little bit of time and space, or a desire to do something, like go for a walk or a run. Whatever they require, we can bring our willingness and acceptance without judging them and their needs.

Co-regulation can be used in moments of distress and upset, but I also like to think of it as something that happens as part of our day-to-day relationships. We are conscious of our partners' nervous systems, and we put effort and intention into not activating it. We can show appreciation and love for our partners, we are kind and considerate, we are helpful and we are playful. All of this maintains a regulated nervous system and thereby gives us the best chance of having a happy and fulfilling partnership.

Regulation and co-regulation mean we have more fuel in the tank when conflicts arise, we are not so quick to react, and there is significantly more mutual trust that we are on each other's side. This is a huge gift of secure relationships and very much worth putting the effort in to achieve.

Those of us with insecure attachment are extremely sensitive to the moods and energy of the people around us, including our environment. Therefore, a part of co-regulation is also taking responsibility for what we are emanating out into our relationships. Can we be moody and grumpy sometimes? Can we be silent, but in a powerful way? Can we say certain things, or give our partners a look, and know that this will be disrupting the calm equilibrium of the relationship? We have a huge impact on the environment of our relationship and, as we have seen, we can take responsibility for what we are putting out there.

Breathing together

Practising breathing exercises with our partners can improve our relationship bond and emotional connection, promoting intimacy and acceptance. A wonderful part of co-regulation, breathing together allows your nervous systems to speak to each other.

BACK BREATHING

- Sit cross-legged on the floor with your backs against one another, hands resting comfortably on the floor, or on your knees or thighs.
- Initially focus on your own body and your own breath.
- As you breathe, relax your shoulders away from your ears, expand your chest, elongate your back and find a comfortable resting place for your body.
- Now start tuning in to your partner's body – how it feels against your back, the skin and the sounds you can hear.
- Keep your breath as natural as possible as you breathe with your partner.
- Start tuning in to your partner's breath more and slowly begin breathing together.

HEART HUG BREATHING

- For increased intimacy, sit on a bed or sofa, facing one another. One person wraps their legs around their partner, over their thighs, with the other person's legs under their partner's thighs.

- Start by holding your heads close to each other with your hand gently on your chest, so you can feel your heart and your breath.
- Both breathe in for the count of five, hold for the count of five and exhale for the count of seven. Repeat.
- After a minute or two, place your hand on their chest and their hand on your chest, feeling each other's hearts. You are now connected to one another's breath more directly.
- It is good to start with your eyes closed, and as your intimacy and comfortableness increases you can open your eyes, looking at each other as you do the exercise.
- Do this for as long as feels comfortable.
- Finish with an embrace, when both your bodies are relaxed and calm and a connection has been built.

Arjun and Anika could be fiery together, and while this worked well for them in the bedroom, there were times when their hot-headedness went too far. Now that Anika was pregnant, they were realising they needed to get on top of their anxiety and arguing. Arjun liked practising the helicopter view (page 170), as considering how things might appear objectively appealed to his rational way of thinking. During difficult conversations, Anika had suggested they pause and do back breathing (page 177) together to stop things getting too heated and because she liked the physical contact. They realised how bonding this could be and it helped them have a much calmer pregnancy.

Distress Tolerance

Further DBT skills fall under the category of distress tolerance, which offers short-term relief from our reactions to difficult, uncomfortable or unpleasant situations. It helps us to stay in charge of our behaviour and not be impulsive or reactive in our relationships. It focuses heavily on accepting reality rather than approving of reality, which reduces our pain and suffering and helps us be more resilient when faced with the inescapable challenges of our lives and partnerships. We can tolerate distress better and not act out unhelpfully.

Radical acceptance

The distress tolerance skill 'radical acceptance' is regarded by many as one of the most challenging of all DBT practices. Acceptance is not easy for many of us, especially when our partners and relationships present us with so much to be unhappy about. This skill suggests we have four options when presented with a problem or pain:

1. We can explore possible solutions.
2. We can change how we feel about the problem.
3. **We can accept the situation.**
4. We can do nothing about it and stay miserable.

You may, for example, accept that your partner doesn't like the cold but then get very upset if they don't swim in the sea with you. That means you've not accepted it. Radical acceptance means total acceptance of all aspects of the situation. It means accepting deeply and completely, so we don't cause ourselves unnecessary distress. Accepting our partners and our circumstances does not mean we condone certain behaviour or approve of what's happening.

Acceptance means we can live in the reality of what's happening – which often opens us up to more solution-focused ways of thinking. Acceptance takes the drama out of situations and it removes the emotional heat from our responses. It is a very useful skill to develop.

Both anxiously attached and avoidantly attached individuals can struggle to practise acceptance, especially of each other. When our insecure attachment is triggered, we become defensive and our attention is on the other person and their faults and failings. The last thing we want to do is accept them or the situation, even if it is for our own benefit. Being in fight mode, we might consider acceptance as 'losing' or 'letting our partners get away with stuff', both of which are not accurate. Acceptance helps us move out of survival mode and focus on the solution rather than the problem.

Wise mind

Another distress tolerance skill is 'wise mind'. DBT suggests that there are various parts of our mind including:

- The rational mind, which is driven by logic and viewing things very practically.
- The emotion mind, which is driven by feelings.

Many of us have a dominant part of the mind. Our rational mind can be overdeveloped and we are highly logical in our approach to life, priding ourselves on being rational and level-headed at all times. Or our emotion mind can be overdeveloped and our way of interacting with the world is highly emotional. In times of distress or upset, our emotions can take over and we are led by our heightened feelings. Both of these minds are extremely important and have a place, but if we are living in one in isolation we are imbalanced.

We are only wise when we are able to incorporate both parts of our mind. The wise mind does not believe that rationality is everything, nor does it believe that emotions are everything. It understands both work together to bring about the best and most healthy – wise – way of approaching things.

From an attachment perspective, the wise mind prevents us from going too far into our emotionality and escalating our anxiety, or too far into our rationality and exacerbating our avoidance. It suggests that true wisdom comes from being connected to our feelings and by being able to access our rationality and practicality, too.

If you are avoidantly attached, the challenge here is to recognise when you are not taking your emotions into account. You might be comfortable living in your head, intellectualising life and dodging feelings; you can also be judgemental about feelings and people who have feelings. If you or your partner notice you are shutting down, challenge yourself and ask yourself these questions:

- What might I be feeling right now?
- What is my behaviour saying about how I feel?

If you are anxiously attached, the challenge here is to recognise when your emotions are ruling you. Perhaps you are feeling overwhelmed or you are unable to think straight. This is a clue that you've gone too far into your emotion mind and need to reduce your upset and tune in to your rational mind to help ground you and calm you. Your emotions are very important but when they take over you have lost control. Even though it feels very compelling to stay in your emotion energy, you can remind yourself to be wise – and to incorporate other parts of your mind that can help. You can remind yourself that your goal is to stay constructive in your relationship, which means calming your emotions and allowing a rational and logical mind to inform you on the next best step.

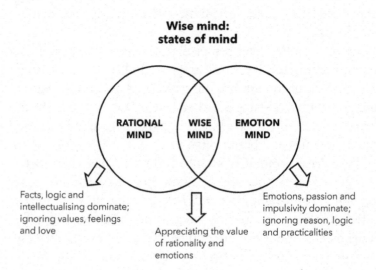

**Wise mind:
states of mind**

RATIONAL MIND

WISE MIND

EMOTION MIND

Facts, logic and intellectualising dominate; ignoring values, feelings and love

Appreciating the value of rationality and emotions

Emotions, passion and impulsivity dominate; ignoring reason, logic and practicalities

A big part of accountability and taking responsibility for ourselves is taking responsibility for our reactions. When we are emotionally dysregulated we will react in ways that are supremely unhelpful and will only exacerbate our insecure ways of attaching. It reinforces our fears and perpetuates our patterns. Taking responsibility for our reactivity and our behaviour when we are activated can be absolutely transformative to our lives and partnerships.

By keeping our emotions stable, we are then able to tackle another crucial part of our relational distress: distorted thinking, which is the focus of the next chapter.

Journalling prompts

- When has emotional dysregulation caused you problems? Give examples.
- How have you felt when you lost control or behaved in ways that were not healthy or helpful?
- Do you have resistance to regulating your emotions?
- What does emotional dysregulation mean to you (angry and explosive, shutting down and withdrawing, feeling uneasy, being passive or aggressive, having a permanently activated nervous system)?
- Which of the tools described above will help you stay in the window of tolerance?

CHAPTER 8

Challenging Distorted Thinking

I t's essential to recognise that insecure attaching and relating is maintained by extreme thinking. If we examine the thoughts that run through our minds, the assumptions, imaginings and projections when we are in an either anxious or avoidant space, we can clearly see how fear-based and extreme they are in nature.

It's important for us to acknowledge this because when we think or feel something, we tend not to question it. A key part of our learning and moving towards secure attachment is fully recognising we cannot trust our thoughts. And when our insecure attachment is activated, we especially cannot trust our thinking. When we are stressed and insecure we can have unhelpful and often highly destructive thoughts about our partners and our relationships, imagining all manner of negative conclusions. This is when our programming is really coming into play. We can character assassinate our partners – and ourselves too. We tip into hopelessness and despair, or we ramp up and go into grandiosity, (or both).

Therefore, a crucial piece of work is around understanding our distorted thinking. Cognitive distortions play a large role in our relationships and are something we all experience – and for those of us with insecure attachment, our thought processes can be very skewed to the negative. **If we are anxiously attached** we can think catastrophic thoughts about our relationships ending or self-defeating thoughts about our lovability and self-worth. **If we are avoidantly attached** we can think in overly rational ways that negate emotion or human need.

We live not in reality but in the constructs of our mind, which means we are coming from a place where all our subjective fears, insecurities, worries and coping mechanisms create a compelling version of what we imagine is taking place. It's vital that you understand the unhelpful thinking styles and extreme thinking that might be happening consciously and unconsciously for you.

These are deeply ingrained in us but, with time and perseverance, we can rewire our brains away from distorted thinking to a more mature, accurate thinking. This chapter will give you the tools to achieve and maintain this mental resilience.

Signs of distorted thinking in your relationship

- It's a struggle for you to think of positives regarding your relationship.
- You think about your partner in very pessimistic or rigid ways.
- There is a lack of compassion and empathy in the partnership.
- Due to defensiveness, arguments happen frequently, with no resolution.
- You feel misunderstood or misrepresented by your partner.

- Blame passes back and forth between you and your partner.
- There is a belief that 'someone's right and someone's wrong'.
- Mistakes and errors are focused on, while demonstrations of love are ignored or dismissed.

Observing Our Thoughts

In learning to recognise when our thinking is becoming extreme, we must first learn how to observe our thoughts. We can develop the skill of noticing what we're thinking and see how that impacts how we behave and relate. *And it's when we are least inclined to do this that it's most important we do.* The hallmark of extreme thinking, after all, is how convinced we are of something. Sometimes, the more sure we are (usually given away by self-righteousness or a sense of impending doom because we 'know' things are about to end in tears), the more we have to do the very hard work of reining ourselves in and examining these so-called certainties.

I encourage you to get curious when you are overly emotional: what gets under your skin, makes you react, explode or implode? These are all very helpful to discover as these are responses that control us, and are often serving to confirm negative parts of our stories and the roles we play in our relationships, not to mention our deepest hurts and fears. This is part of our awareness-raising, so we can understand better why we do what we do.

Questioning our thoughts

We have a lot of inaccurate thoughts when it comes to our partners and relationships. Therapies such as cognitive behavioural therapy (CBT) and rational emotive behaviour therapy (REBT - see page 198) are very useful because they teach us to notice our irrational thoughts, apprehend those thoughts, and replace negative thoughts with more accurate ones.

Questioning our thoughts is a very useful habit to develop. There are many cognitive distortions and thinking errors that take place in our brains every day, but we seldom stop to reflect on how helpful they are or the role they might be playing in continuing our difficulty and perpetuating our patterns.

CBT teaches us that what we think and feel often has an impact on how we behave. Therefore, by understanding our cognitions (our perceptions, ideas and mental processes) better, and making conscious efforts to keep them constructive and in line with our values and goals, so too will our behaviour become healthier. CBT believes that our actions and cognitions are interrelated, and therefore, focusing on our cognitions is a key part of behavioural change.

Unhelpful Thinking Styles

What are the unhelpful thinking errors we can make, especially when it comes to our partnerships? Consider the list overleaf and check off any you recognise. We all do these to some degree and, if they are a rare occurrence, they are not cause for concern. However, many of us experience unhelpful thinking styles regularly, sometimes on a daily basis, and it is therefore key that we begin to recognise these errors so we can course-correct and help ourselves and our relationships by doing things differently.

Magnification and minimisation

This is where we exaggerate (magnify and maximise) or minimise the importance of events. You might believe your needs are unimportant or that your mistakes are excessively important. Or you might magnify the positive attributes of other people and minimise your own. You may bury your head in the sand when there are problems in your relationship or you may overreact to small, human errors.

Catastrophising

This is seeing only the worst possible outcome of a situation. You might imagine your relationship ending or your partner being unfaithful. You may also label situations as terrible, outrageous or 'the worst'. When we catastrophise we are having a disproportionate response to what's happening and also imagining the worst if we're looking to the future.

Overgeneralisation

Language like 'always' and 'never' gives this away. We might make broad statements about things, often ignoring the good or focusing on the small details to prove our expectations. Due to our stories and narratives (see page 51), we can think 'all people are untrustworthy', 'no one will ever love me' and so on. Often rooted in abandonment and trauma, this is unhelpful because we paint the whole world and everyone in it with the same brush, not leaving room for nuance or new experiences.

Jumping to conclusions

Remember our brains like order and repetition, so once we 'know' someone, we are in danger of jumping to conclusions and interpreting the meaning of a situation without sufficient evidence. We might make assumptions or project into the future, not realising we are in our head rather than in the here-and-now of the present experience.

Personalisation

This is when we hold ourselves personally responsible for an event that is not entirely under our control. For example, feeling shame or guilt when a partner behaves badly. It's also when we make things about us when they're not, like if a loved one is going through a tough time and we talk to everyone about how hard it is for us.

Mind reading

'That person hates me', 'They think I'm stupid', 'She can't be bothered with me' are all examples of mind reading. We might imagine we know what other people are thinking and often judge ourselves through other people's eyes. We think we can interpret the thoughts and beliefs of others without them telling us directly.

Fortune telling (predicting the future)

This is similar to mind reading, except it is about the future in a more general way. You might expect certain outcomes without any appropriate evidence or information. This can be in a catastrophising way, such as 'They're going to break my heart', or in a fantasy way, such as 'Once we're together, everything will be perfect.'

Disqualifying the positive (having a 'mental filter')

As the name suggests, this is when we recognise only the negative aspects of a situation or relationship, while ignoring the positive. Our lives are interpreted through a mental filter which removes the good, hopeful or validating aspects of our interactions or relationships. For example, we might receive many affirmations from loved ones but focus on one single piece of negative feedback.

Emotional reasoning

This is a hugely unconscious process and is an important one to recognise. We base our view of situations or ourselves on the way we are feeling. Our way of working things out is through our emotions. While our emotions are important, they are also highly subjective and rooted in our fears and insecurities. In the extreme, they often lack perspective, proportion or objectivity. This is part of reactivity and jumping to conclusions, when we have big feelings and behave impulsively in the heat of the moment.

Labelling

Labelling is deeply unhelpful and compromising to our esteem or view of others. You might describe yourself or others by making global statements based on limited evidence, ignoring examples that aren't consistent with our pronouncement. For example, 'I'm stupid', 'They're lazy', 'You're selfish.'

All-or-nothing thinking

Similar to overgeneralisation, all-or-nothing thinking is when we view life and people in absolutes, seeing only one extreme or the other. Situations or loved ones are either good or bad, wrong or right. You might use words like 'always', 'never' or 'every'. There are no in-betweens or shades of grey. You have tunnel vision and struggle to appreciate nuance or complexity.

How can we create a new reality for ourselves when we are so certain of negative outcomes? If we are continually feeding the insatiable appetite of our negativity, how, precisely, is it going to reduce? It is completely understandable to worry sometimes and consider what could go wrong. The problem with this mindset, however, is the messaging inherent in it. We are saying to ourselves: only the negatives matter. We are only going to consider the negatives. We will not think of positives – faith, hope, learning and growth – we will anticipate the worst. Doom is the only possible outcome we will accommodate.

By catastrophising, not only are we fortune telling, we are priming ourselves. It doesn't get more self-defeatist than this. We are telling ourselves that things will be bad. This has become reality in our minds, not possibility. So now we are living in this painful, esteem-destroying and depressing distorted reality.

What an injustice this is to ourselves. By throwing petrol on the small flame of our fear, it doesn't take very long before we have created a bonfire. We have been frightened for too long and fear is at the centre of every one of our thoughts. Our brain has changed shape to prioritise and anticipate the fear.

The Skill of Detachment

By taking an emotional step away from our thoughts we can begin to learn to detach from them – we can be observers of our thoughts, not dominated by them. Just because we think things, it doesn't really mean anything. Human beings have over 80,000 thoughts a day and research shows the majority of those are negative. We need to get into the habit of allowing our thoughts to happen but not giving them too much meaning.

As we notice the thoughts, we can begin to think, 'Oh, here I am worrying about this again' or 'I notice I am imagining this terrible thing happening.' As we detach from our thoughts, we create space between us and what we think, so we can bring in more helpful thinking processes. We can question how healthy they are, so we can acknowledge them as intrusive thoughts and therefore thoughts we need to be wary of, rather than swallow whole. We cannot trust our thoughts. Thoughts don't mean anything at all. What we think doesn't matter; what we do does.

We can shift our focus away from the importance of our thoughts to the importance of what we are doing instead. This is where we begin to exercise choice. We can focus on doing some of the suggestions outlined in Chapter 7, regardless of what is going on in our head. Positive action is much more significant than negative thoughts.

The Agony of Ruminating

Do you ever think the same things over and over on a loop? Do you have the same thoughts, which tend to be sad or negative, in prolonged and intense ways? We all have repetitive thoughts sometimes, but rumination is when we get stuck in a cycle and it is difficult for us to get out of it. Our thoughts can become like a runaway train and we lose control of what we are thinking and how much we are thinking. This can have a big impact on how we feel and how we behave, and, if our ruminations are pertaining to our partners or relationships, how we relate to the people we care about.

Five ways to help break the cycle of rumination

1. DISTRACT YOURSELF

When you notice you are ruminating, finding a distraction can break your thought cycle temporarily. When we distract ourselves, it allows us to press pause on our thoughts and can also help us to redirect them to something more helpful and likely to achieve our goals. You could:

- call a friend or family member
- do something practical, like home admin
- devote some time to self-care, such as going for a walk, listening to a podcast or doing a guided meditation (see page 158 for more on self-care)
- engage in your favourite form of art
- read a book that is escapist and captures your attention

2. MAKE A PLAN

Often, we are ruminating about things that are out of our control. You can remind yourself what is within your control and make a plan to tackle that.

For example, if you are concerned about your partner being away visiting family, you can recognise that you only have control over yourself and create a schedule for the days your partner is away, where you see friends, participate in stress-relieving exercise, eat healthily, get enough rest and care for yourself with kindness.

3. CHALLENGE YOUR THOUGHTS

We can be at the mercy of our thoughts, not realising we need to learn to question them. When we are having repetitive thoughts, we lack perspective. By questioning our thoughts, reality-checking them and right-sizing our reactions, we can break the cycle and try to take back a bit more control.

4. REMEMBER YOUR GOAL

It's always helpful to come back to our goals. For those of us who struggle with insecure attachment, people-pleasing, perfectionism and other stress-related processes, we can remember goals such as trying to stay healthy, remaining in the middle ground and not having extremes in thinking or behaving. Reminding ourselves of our goals can motivate us to do the actions necessary to interrupt our thoughts and break the cycle (you will be setting goals at the end of this book – see page 309).

These goals also spur us on to exercise and be healthy, do some journalling, use emotional regulation techniques (see Chapter 7), practise mindfulness and meditation, and whatever else works to soothe our distressing thoughts.

5. UNDERSTAND WHAT TRIGGERS YOUR RUMINATION

Self-awareness is all-important, so we can catch rumination early. Often, certain fears or assumptions trigger a rumination cycle and it's useful to troubleshoot ahead of time if you know you're going into triggering territory. For example, if you know seeing a certain person or certain circumstances can bring up some anxiety or fear in you, you can catch rumination before it starts. You can be mindful and resist the hamster wheel of negative rumination.

You can use all these skills to stay steady, knowing that rumination isn't constructive or helpful and can cause significant suffering. Research shows that if we catch rumination early, that is the most helpful time to redirect our focus. Once we've been ruminating for a long time, breaking the cycle becomes harder. So do your best to know your triggers so you can catch yourself early.

Negative Beliefs Around Relationships

Our belief system is what we have learnt about relationships and will impact our attitude to others, assumptions we will make about other people and our relationships, and the partnerships we expect to have. Our beliefs are incredibly powerful because they form the basis of how we relate and what we will create for ourselves in our partnerships (see Chapter 2). If we have an insecure attachment style, we can have some unhelpful beliefs about ourselves and relationships. This is part of our distorted thinking and often requires us to update our beliefs to ones that are more optimistic and hopeful.

Having awareness of our beliefs is an important part of rewiring our attachment, because our core beliefs drive our behaviour and ways of relating. Becoming more secure means developing more secure beliefs. Secure beliefs are:

- believing that people are fundamentally good
- believing we are able to cope and deal with difficulty in our partnerships

- believing we will recognise if things are not right for us and will walk away from relationships that are unhealthy
- believing we are worthy of love
- believing healthy relationships are possible and preferable

Now let's examine some negative beliefs you might have. Again, these are often deeply unconscious and therefore out of your awareness. But you can look at your previous relationships and what is taking place in your relationship today to see if some of these beliefs might be playing out:

- 'I need to control the other person or they'll control me.'
- 'I mustn't trust anyone. Relationships are dangerous.'
- 'My needs don't matter.'
- 'I am not worthy of love.'
- 'I can't trust anyone.'
- 'Love will be easy with the right person.'
- 'I have to sacrifice for love.'
- 'I'll never meet anyone who lives up to my standards.'

These are just a small number of possible negative beliefs you might have. It is worth spending some time on this and giving thought to it in order to recognise what you are bringing to your relationship.

Opposite are some journalling questions so you can do some reflection work and uncover your negative beliefs. Choose one and do some word association. Without thinking about things too deeply, and certainly without trying to get the answer right, simply write down what comes to mind when you first read the question. Give yourself several minutes to write, in a stream of consciousness way, to see what is revealed. When you have finished, highlight the sentences that feel the most powerful for you. These might reveal the negative beliefs you need to challenge and grow out of.

- Do you feel special in relationships? Explore.
- What are the first thoughts you have when considering the availability of love in your relationships?
- Write down your immediate reaction when asking yourself the question: what happens in relationships for me?
- Contemplate what you have learnt about love. Is it easy to get? Is it unconditional? Is it tender and gentle? What words would you use?

Chloe prided herself on being a strong woman – she was ambitious and knew what she wanted. However, when it came to her partner, she was secretive and felt overwhelmed with worry a lot of the time. She was convinced he was about to leave her and that if she showed anything less than a sexy, fun, carefree, powerful woman he would be disappointed and move on to someone 'better'. Sometimes she imagined him with other women, even in bed, having a great time, and compared herself very unfavourably to these imaginary goddesses.

Realising that her parents' infidelities had left her feeling very sexually insecure in relationships, she was able to reframe her fears and bring compassion and clarity to her distorted thoughts. She recognised that, rather than feeding her negative thoughts and exacerbating her fears, she needed to reassure herself with kinder thoughts and focus more on reality and healing.

Shoulds and Musts

REBT (rational emotive behavioural therapy) is a form of CBT that brings our focus to some very significant cognitive distortions. This form of psychotherapy is built on the premise that it is not the events in our lives that cause emotions but rather our beliefs that cause us to experience what Albert Ellis, the founder of REBT, describes as unhealthy negative emotions, such as anger, anxiety, disappointment or jealousy. It challenges us to consider and change our irrational beliefs, so we can reduce emotional pain and interpersonal distress. The work encourages us to become aware of when we are being rigid and inflexible. Ellis posited we can be too extreme in our attitudes and we place demands on ourselves and other people that are unrealistic and unhelpful. We can recognise this behaviour by noticing irrational thoughts, which contain 'musts' or 'shoulds'.

When experiencing an unhealthy negative emotion, we can bring our attention to what we might be demanding from ourselves or our partners. If we are feeling angry, for example, we can question: what about our partners or situations evoked anger in us, and what are we therefore demanding from them to elicit such a reaction in us?

Perhaps we were demanding:

- My partner must not behave in ways that I do not like.
- My partner must do what I want, how I want it.
- My partner must not have their own opinion.
- My partner should not do that.
- I should not have to explain this to my partner.
- My partner should do as I say.

When we can see the demands underneath our unhealthy negative emotions, we can recognise that we are being inflexible and unrealistic in what we want from our part-ners. Often, we are exerting our own will on them and thereby creating emotional upset in ourselves. The REBT philosophy is encapsulated by Epictetus' saying: 'Men are disturbed not by things but by the view they take of them.'

REBT teaches us to move away from the rigid, inflexible demands of musts, shoulds, oughts and should nots, and instead use more moderate and realistic language such as, 'I would like . . .', 'I would love . . .' or 'I would prefer . . .'

For example, instead of 'My partner must agree with me' we can de-intensify it from a demand to a preference: 'I would love my partner to agree with me all the time but I realise that is not realistic. We agree on many things, but we can disagree on certain things and I can cope with that.' Or: 'I would prefer my partner to agree with me on all things. However, I understand they are their own person and may have different opinions at times.' This takes away the extreme thinking of these moments, reminding us to loosen our grip and to be more philosophical and respectful in our approach.

Can you recognise where you are placing demands on yourself, your partner and your relationship? It is appropri-ate and healthy to want things from our partnerships and to work on issues; however, demands can actually get in the way of genuine discussion and progress.

How to Reframe Unhelpful Thoughts

Once we start recognising negative thoughts and noticing when we are having them, we are able to bring in the CBT skill of reframing our thoughts. By challenging and learning to replace these thoughts, we help ourselves move away from stress and anxiety to better mental and emotional health. By noticing our thoughts, we are able to take a step back, pause and then continue in a way that is more helpful.

Recognise your unhelpful thoughts

Often, we are not even aware we are thinking in an unhelpful way. We need to bring our attention to what's going on in our mind and recognise when it is unhelpful.

You can look out for:

- When you are always expecting the worst.
- Negating the good and over-focusing on the negative.
- Engaging in all-or-nothing thinking.
- Thinking about yourself, your partner or your relationship in purely negative ways.

Practise catching your negative thoughts

When you notice your thoughts, you can get better at catching them. Being able to catch yourself in a negative loop or unhelpful spiral means you can apprehend your thoughts and start reflecting on them more.

Examine your unhelpful thoughts

Our unhelpful thinking patterns often go unchecked by us. We agree with our negative projections and our fears, believe them to be completely valid, and, if we're not careful, will soon be catastrophising and believing the worst. Instead, we need to reality-check and right-size them in our hearts and minds.

Ways to examine your thoughts include:

- Look for evidence to prove your thoughts.
- Ask yourself whether your thoughts are based on information or imagination.
- Question how proportionate your thoughts are.

- Ask yourself if your best friend would agree with your thoughts.
- Ascertain if thinking like this is beneficial to you and likely to help you be happy and healthy.

Reframe your thoughts

This is when you can take a distorted thought and change it to something more accurate. Having questioned your thoughts, reality-checked them and right-sized them, now you can reframe them in a way that will be healthy and constructive.

Some examples of cognitive reframes include:

Distorted thought: 'My partner always forgets special occasions.'

Reframe: 'I know my partner doesn't place the same importance on special occasions as I do. They show their love to me through acts of service.'

Distorted thought: 'I am a failure at relationships.'

Reframe: 'I've had some tough relationship experiences but I'm determined to get the love I deserve.'

Anxiously attached beliefs reframe

Below are some examples of reframing our anxious thoughts and beliefs to something more realistic and helpful:

- 'I might struggle with having space away from my partner in relationships sometimes; however, it does not mean I am not loved.'
- 'Even if there is not intensity with my partner, I know I am okay.'

- 'Being assertive (rather than passive or aggressive) can be challenging for me; however, I am learning to do so every day.'
- 'There are always negative things in a relationship. I must be mindful to appreciate and value the good and positive things too.'
- 'When anxiety or worry comes up for me, I can lovingly tend to that part of myself, self-soothe and bring myself the security I need.'

Avoidantly attached beliefs reframe

Below are some examples of reframing our avoidant thoughts and beliefs to something more realistic and helpful:

- 'If there is closeness in a relationship it does not mean I am unsafe.'
- 'Intense connection can be challenging but I can do it for short periods.'
- 'When I feel put upon or demands are being made of me it might be painful, but I can cope and desensitise to engaging with life and other people more.'
- 'I cannot trust my thinking when over-focusing on the negatives of my partner and relationship.'
- 'When I feel angry or irritated it might be because of someone else (and what I think they need to change), but I can stay focused on myself and keeping my behaviour healthy and loving.'

Shift your perspective

How we think, our attitudes and our outlook should not be underestimated. Take some time to consider the scenario below:

I wake up and I'm furious with you. Your snoring and tossing and turning disturbed me all night as usual, and I'm exhausted. When I walk past you as you're getting dressed, I let you know how you ruined my night. In the car, your music choices are so bad and I tell you so. You put your hand on my thigh and I wonder how you could possibly think touching me in that way is appropriate right now. I stare out the window, half angry, half teary behind my sunglasses, wondering why you can't love me better. We get to our friend's home. I can't wait to catch up with everyone and get some space from you. One of our friends is in the honeymoon phase of her relationship and I tell her to enjoy it while it lasts. I tell a few funny stories about you, about your ineptitude and failings, and make everyone laugh, like I always do.

As we leave, I roll my eyes when a friend tells me to enjoy the rest of our day together. Driving home you're silent, acting upset. I despise you for this.

When we get home, I want to relax and read, and you want to do some spring cleaning together. We bicker about this, then I go and read while you clean the kitchen. I marvel at how you are able to make almost every interaction unpleasant.

After a couple of hours and a nap, it's clear you're not going to apologise. I think about how petty and immature you are, and question this relationship for the millionth time.

We decide to take the dog for a walk. While we wander around our neighbourhood, you talk about your struggles at work. I'm annoyed because it's always about you. Why am I always hearing about your life? And the work struggles!

They're never-ending. I lecture you about what to do, as I always do, and we walk in silence till we get home. You don't ask me a single thing about me and my life. Here I am, supporting you and helping you, and you can't even be bothered to ask me about me. This is such a one-sided relationship.

As we get ready for bed, you are completely in the way in the bathroom, which riles me. Don't you know how much I hate having two people in our small bathroom? When we get into bed, you start tickling my legs and acting cute, which I know is your pathetic attempt at trying to initiate sex. There's nothing I want less. I cut you dead and roll over onto my side. I'm so sad. Where is this relationship going? Am I meant to be this unhappy?

Let's now explore an alternative scenario:

I wake up and I'm so sleepy. I can see you're getting dressed and I call you over to me. You come and sit on the side of the bed; we smile at each other, kiss and say good morning.

'Your snoring was quite bad again last night,' I report.

'Oh no,' you say, with a guilty face.

In the car, your music choices are so bad, they make me laugh. I decide to be in charge of the music. You put your hand on my thigh and I put my hand on yours. I stare out the window watching the world go by as we chat and listen to music together. We get to our friend's home and I can't wait to catch up with everyone. One of our friends is in the honeymoon phase of her relationship and I tell her if she puts in the work, it just gets better and better. I regale everyone with a few funny stories about us, about our hectic lives and naughty dog. As the day progresses, we gravitate to sitting next to each other, our bodies close.

As we leave, I wink at my friend when she tells me to enjoy the rest of our day together. Driving home we're in high spirits, having had a fun lunch. I love us when we're like this.

When we get home, I want to relax and read, and you want to do some spring cleaning. I hate spring cleaning, so we agree to do that for an hour and then I can go and read. I'm so grateful we can come to a compromise easily. After sorting out the house, we're hot and dusty, so have a quick shower and end up having sex on the bed with the windows open and a cool breeze coming in. You leave me to nap with our little dog and I couldn't be more content.

When I wake up, we decide to take the dog for a walk. While we wander around our neighbourhood you tell me about your work. I love it when you share things with me, so I ask lots of questions and remind you how brilliant you are at what you do. I share some stuff about my life, laughing about my family, who you know all about, and describe the latest drama. As we walk, we hold hands. This is such a relaxed relationship.

As we get ready for bed, you are completely in the way in the bathroom which riles me! You know how much I hate having two people in our small bathroom, but you tease me and joke with me, and laugh away my grumpiness. When we get into bed, you start tickling my legs and acting cute. We cuddle for 20 minutes before turning out the light. I love feeling the warmth of your body.

As I drift off to sleep, I hear you breathing steadily and remember the many years I was lonely in my bed. Our happy little life means everything to me.

Our perspective is extremely powerful. The very nature of our attachment styles are about how we view things. They determine how we interpret things, how we project things and how we relate to things. The difficulties of an intimate relationship can distort our perspectives very easily.

Shifting our perspective is both easy and extremely difficult. It's easy because we are in control of it. We can notice our thoughts, train our brains towards appreciation, the good, being unconditional, being accepting. It can be a daily practice.

But it is extremely difficult because our unconscious, automatic responses are constant. When we're in a relationship with someone, when we're sharing our lives with one another, every moment presents an opportunity to be unconsciously negative or consciously proactive. It is extremely effortful to be loving. It takes years of effort, to make that habit.

Use a thought record

If you have a lot of unhelpful negative thoughts, it is very useful to use a thought record (see below). This is a short, simple daily exercise that allows you to keep a record of the negative thoughts you have and for you to chart your development as you challenge and reframe your thoughts. You can see which are the most pervasive thoughts and also notice that things are slowly improving.

Prompt	Example	My thought
1. What happened?	My partner let me down.	
2. My reactive feelings	Frustrated, angry, disappointed.	
3. Unhelpful thoughts I had	They don't get anything right. They are useless.	
4. Evidence to support my unhelpful thoughts	They've let me down many times before.	
5. Evidence against my unhelpful thoughts	Nobody is perfect and we all let each other down all the time. There are many things my partner does for me that are wonderful that I don't always acknowledge or appreciate.	

Prompt	Example	My thought
6. More accurate thoughts or reframes	My partner let me down in this instance. I don't need to make a bigger deal out of it than it is. They are good to me in many other ways.	
7. What are my feelings now I've reflected?	I'm feeling calmer. Also happy I'm being accepting and kind.	

When we have greater awareness of how distorted our thinking can be and how to keep our thoughts and beliefs constructive, we can begin to think about communicating in ways that are both respectful and effective. We'll explore this in the next chapter.

Journalling prompts

- When you stop to observe your thoughts, can you recognise negative, extreme, distorted thinking? What are these thoughts?
- Which of the unhelpful thinking styles on page 200 can you recognise?
- Do you ruminate, having certain worries going round your head on a loop? What are they?
- Can you recognise the negative beliefs around relationships that are at the root of your distorted thinking? What are they?
- Which tools explored in this chapter appeal to you?

CHAPTER 9

Healthy Communication

Many of us have numerous problems when it comes to communication. We have a problem with listening. We have a problem with expressing our needs simply and directly. We have a problem with accountability. We have a problem with emotions. We have a problem with our partners' emotions. We have a problem with talking too much. We have a problem with not talking enough.

Communication is very significant because it encapsulates whether we are acknowledged and heard. How we are communicated with can help us feel respected and cared for, or it can render us feeling hurt and invalidated. And how we express ourselves can boost our self-esteem, by being composed, mature and sincere, or it can keep us stuck in negative loops of blame and repetitive arguing that erode our self-worth and any tenderness in the relationship.

Communication skills are just that – skills, which we need to learn and develop. Communication is more than just speaking. It's active listening, it's thinking before responding, it's affirming each other, and it's getting our thoughts and feelings across in appropriate and effective ways.

We can reveal our unhealthy beliefs around communication when we think or say things like:

- 'Why can't I just say what I feel?'
- 'I'm only being honest.'
- 'I'd rather say nothing and keep the peace.'
- 'I'm not the one with communication problems, they are.'

When we are anxiously attached, we can often fall into the first point and over-explain, sharing our thought processes, feelings and reactions in a very granular way, as an attempt to meet our need of being understood.

When we are avoidantly attached, we often use honesty as a way of expressing ourselves in overly blunt and abrasive ways, as an attempt to meet our need of being heard, while also expressing some of our anger.

Saying nothing or being silent is both **an anxious and an avoidant behaviour.** When **avoidant,** we'll try to dodge serious conversations and be unresponsive in order to keep the peace; when **anxious,** we will choose not to say things for fear of rocking the boat or being rejected.

Finally, it is easier to blame or find fault with our partners and how they communicate or things they said than it is to reflect on our own ways of communicating or things we said that were less than helpful. As long as we're pointing the finger at our partners, we abdicate responsibility. Which means that what is happening in the relationship is unlikely to change.

How readily we go to our partners for support and how safe we feel to share in our relationships shows the level of communicative skill within the partnership. Rather than feeling ease and confidence, we can feel the need to walk on eggshells, censor ourselves, or be prone to explosions because we've been bottling up our emotions.

When it comes to expressing ourselves to our partners – especially in times of upset or anger – many of us fall into the passive or aggressive categories.

In our attempts to get what we want we can be passive:

- people-pleasing
- self-sacrificing
- quiet
- dependent

Or we can be aggressive:

- controlling
- critical
- angry
- loud
- domineering

If we have been too passive for too long, we can snap and then become aggressive in our approach. Likewise, if we are too aggressive at times, we can feel guilty and then become passive as a way of compensating.

Neither of these are viable long-term ways of relating in our partnerships. But there is another way . . .

Learning to Be Assertive

Being passive or aggressive may feel natural, but ultimately it is not constructive or esteeming. Assertiveness is emotionally intelligent and responsible, which is what will yield the best results and will also enrich our relationships (and relational skills).

Learning to be assertive is a daily practice, as our automatic, insecure ways of relating will have us collapsing into ineffective ways of expressing ourselves very quickly. I suggest challenging yourself to be assertive once every day: this might be making one assertive request, standing up for yourself at work, or telling a server that your order isn't right. This helps us develop the muscle and shows ourselves we can express ourselves simply without any drama.

Recognising passive, aggressive and assertive behaviour

Noticing when we are behaving in one of these three ways of relating and communicating helps us to become more aware of our automatic, unconscious reactions, and whether they are healthy or not. See below some examples of each:

PASSIVE:
- being overly agreeable
- being overly accommodating
- compromising too much
- not speaking up
- not having limits
- being a victim

AGGRESSIVE:
- being overly disagreeable
- being obstructive or combative
- dominating too much
- being rude and unpleasant
- not having any boundaries
- being out of control
- being the villain

ASSERTIVE:
- speaking up for oneself
- having discussions to problem-solve

- being straightforward and transparent about wishes
- maintaining respect for oneself and others
- having appropriate boundaries and expecting other people to as well
- being adult

Examples of communicating in these ways:

PASSIVE:
- 'Things don't work out for me . . .' (feeling powerless)
- 'Don't worry about me!'
- *silence*
- doesn't know how to say no
- speaks softly or weakly

AGGRESSIVE:
- tone is cold, sharp or sarcastic
- 'There's no way I'm doing that'
- 'Do as I say (you know I'm always right)' (domineering)
- struggles to hear other people
- speaks loudly or forcefully

ASSERTIVE:
- tone is curious and open
- 'Here's what I think . . .'
- 'Let's discuss what would be best for everyone'
- 'I am frustrated and I can see you are too. Let's talk about it'
- speaks calmly and confidently

Being assertive is part of being securely attached. We feel secure in ourselves, have sufficient confidence to express ourselves, and have enough respect for ourselves and others to do it in a way that is constructive, rather than inflammatory or defensive.

This chapter explores the many ways we can be assertive in how we communicate and how we can develop communication skills that will manage the fear, anxiety and overwhelm that is part of our anxious or avoidant ways of interacting with others.

When we are anxiously attached, we can swing on the pendulum between passive and aggressive. Sometimes our survival response is to go into fawn, where we people-please and over-function, but after a while we can get resentful and our response changes to fight mode. Then we can forcefully complain and vent in very angry ways.

When we are avoidantly attached, we can also oscillate between passive and aggressive. Passive when we're avoiding, lying low, trying to dodge responsibility, and aggressive when we're in our dismissiveness or fearful avoidance. Then our annoyance lacks boundaries and we can be rude and hostile.

Neither of these options instil trust or safety and it would be beneficial to use the skills in this chapter to develop our assertiveness skills so we can communicate with more care.

The Importance of Non-Verbal Communication

In our partnerships, we are often hyperaware of one another's micro expressions and non-verbal communication. We can easily trigger one another through our tone of voice, facial expressions and body language. We can send clear messages to our partners through these channels, and we need to bring as much attention and care to this as we do to how we are speaking and the words we are choosing. In many instances, it is our non-verbal communication that does most of the talking. The power of what we express without words cannot be underestimated.

We all know the impact of a filthy look, a raised brow or an eye-roll. Our bodies and face can deliver a host of painful and unpleasant messages to our partners, and, when used with certain words and language, can create a relationship-destroying combination.

Try this exercise. Go to a mirror and, recalling a recent upset or disagreement, repeat some of the statements you were saying to your partner in the manner in which you said them. Notice what your expression transmits and what your non-verbal communication was conveying when you were hurt. You might be surprised by just how either meek or harsh you came across. It's useful to see what our partners see. This can give us an understanding of how likely it was that we would have had our needs met in that situation.

How to listen

NOT LISTENING CHECKLIST:

- distracted, not paying attention (e.g., on phone, looking away)
- interrupting, correcting or deflecting
- can't remember what partner said
- shaking head, disagreeing
- face pulling or anxious/tense/angry
- heart is closed and uninterested in what partner is sharing/has already made up mind
- defensive and judgemental
- focused on being right
- pride and ego in charge
- invalidating comments and attitude

LISTENING CHECKLIST:

- facing person speaking, really paying attention
- not interrupting
- repeating back what partner has said
- nodding and making reassuring sounds
- soft in face, eyes and body
- open-hearted and curious
- non-defensive and non-judgemental
- focused on lovingness
- pride and ego in check
- supportive language and statements

None of us are perfect and this is an ambitious list. However, it's important to strive for this level of empathy, compassion and openness. This way of communicating regulates emotions, reduces fears and increases intimacy and good feeling. It is a true act of love.

Communication Clangers

Everyone has bad days and sometimes we say or do the wrong thing. This is human and part of healthy, adult relationships. Unhealthy communication, however, is when unhelpful, unconstructive ways of expressing ourselves have become habit and part of our relational soundtrack.

Overleaf are the many ways in which we can be inadvertently harming our relationships and communicating very ineffectively and indirectly, and how to turn that around.

Note: We will find that we often need to utilise emotional regulation skills in conjunction with these new behaviours.

Criticism

Fault-finding can be addictive. We are all guilty of this some-times but if it has become commonplace we need to break this habit as soon as possible. No one likes to be criticised and, in an intimate relationship, criticism is one of the top relationship-destroying behaviours.

Notice when you're saying things to your partner like, 'You don't ever listen!', 'That's not how you do that', 'Can't you get anything right?', 'That was stupid' – these are the normalised hallmarks of criticism.

Alternatives to criticism include: writing a gratitude list to develop empathy and appreciation (see page 280), training your brain towards the positives, asking questions for clar-ity, understanding that people do things differently, and praising and complimenting your partner's strengths.

Sarcasm

This can be patronising and denigrating and is seldom as funny as we think it is. When we are sarcastic, we are often rude and speak to people in ways we would not appreciate ourselves. We are being superior when we are doing this, which means we are looking down on our partners.

Alternatives to sarcasm include: focusing on your tone of voice, staying neutral and respectful, keeping language appropriate and boundaried, and resisting jibes and 'smart' comments.

Defensiveness

'You're on the same team' is a reminder many of us require regularly. It is very sad how we can make our partners the enemy. Once a pattern of being hurt or disappointed in our relationships is established, who our partners are distorts in our minds and we can, over time, demonise them. They change from being fallible human beings to malicious people hell-bent on making our lives miserable. We lose perspective and fear (and believe) the worst.

In this way, we protect ourselves from taking responsibility for our part in any relationship difficulty. We keep our focus on the other person and their perceived failings, placing ourselves once again in the victim position. If we have felt alone or isolated in our lives, we will recreate this loneliness in our relationships.

Part of blame, defensiveness is when we protect ourselves unnecessarily. When our partners share information with us we are quick to throw it back at them, unable to take responsibility or be accountable. We can then accuse our partners of something in an attempt to deflect from ourselves. Defensiveness reveals our struggle to reflect on our own behaviour, have insight into our own issues, and tolerate ever doing anything wrong, intentional or not.

Alternatives to defensiveness include: taking responsibility, developing active listening skills, staying open to our partners' feedback, recognising when we are going into victim mode, and staying focused on ourself rather than our partners.

Blame versus taking responsibility

We can be extreme in our thinking when we're hurting: someone needs to be the victim and someone needs to be the villain. This is highly unhelpful in the emotionally complex world of relationships. When we fall into this way of thinking, we can become fixated on wanting to be proved right and we are very quick to character assassinate the other person, while ignoring our own failings.

A big part of blame is about wanting what is going on in our relationship to be different and blaming our partners when it's not. But rather than blaming, we can develop the skill of taking responsibility. If things are happening in our relationship that we don't like, we need to take responsibility for speaking out; for sharing with our partners when we feel uncomfortable or hurt; for making requests so our partners can learn what it is we need.

Taking responsibility is about breathing deeply and reflecting on the behaviour we are exhibiting in our relationships and whether it's helpful or unhelpful.

Shaming

To belittle and shame someone for how they're feeling or something they have done is a very sad power move. It can also be dehumanising, as we intentionally want to make someone feel bad about themselves. This will likely be a learnt behaviour from our childhood. It is a form of bullying that is deeply unkind and, at times, abusive.

Alternatives to shaming include: understanding why you do this, recognising if you yourself carry a lot of shame, getting comfortable with vulnerability (your partner's and your own), and working on your ability to be understanding and empathic.

Contempt

This is where a lot of non-verbal communication comes in – things like eye rolling, smirking and parodying. There are so many things wrong when we are being contemptuous: we are condescending, disrespectful, assuming the one-up position and thinking the worst of our partners. Sometimes we can be cruel and downright mean.

Alternatives to contempt include: striving to be understanding, forgiving easily, recognising if you have resentment and dealing with it directly, and focusing on developing appreciation and admiration for your partner.

Control

It's natural to want our partners to do certain things, but we can go overboard and move into micromanaging, dominating and domineering behaviour very easily. We can also become demanding and give unsolicited advice a lot of the time.

If you notice you are telling your partner what to do, correcting them or trying to manage their life for them, you might be controlling.

Alternatives to control include: nurturing a 'live and let live' attitude, working on your acceptance, only giving advice when asked, and focusing on your own life and your own areas for growth.

Name-calling

It is never okay to call someone pathetic, stupid, weak or other slurs. Name-calling is highly critical, invalidates some people and can traumatise others. It is a form of bullying and grandiosity, and needs to be nipped in the bud.

Alternatives to name-calling include: speaking about yourself, having boundaries around what you say, focusing on respecting the other person, and apologising for past name-calling.

It's humbling to recognise the unhealthy behaviour that can play out in our partnerships and how destructive it can be. We can be surprisingly reckless when it comes to our closest relationships, and we end up hurting ourselves and each other enormously. We cannot be securely attached when this is what routinely takes place in our relationships. Secure attachment is about safety and all these behaviours are intrinsically unsafe.

This chapter will give you the skills to be accountable for how you communicate, and you'll learn ways of expressing yourself and your needs that are effective and productive.

Communication skills for anxiety to security

When anxiety says		How to communicate from security
'We don't spend enough time together.'	⇨	'I enjoy spending time with you. Let's do something together.'
'It feels like you don't care about me.'	⇨	'I need reassurance and validation.'
'Why are you so indifferent?'	⇨	'I'm not feeling your love is being demonstrated.'
'Are you committed to me?'	⇨	'Where's my teammate?'
'The kids and I would like more from you.'	⇨	'You are so important to us. Let's refocus on what's important.'
'You're hurting me!'	⇨	'When you _____, it upsets me.'

Communication skills for avoidance to security

When avoidance says		How to communicate from security
'I need some space' (or simply takes space).	⇨	'I need a bit of time to myself, but I still love you.'
'It's not a big deal.'	⇨	'This isn't important to me - I need you to explain why it's important to you.'
'Let's play it by ear.'	⇨	'I don't like making plans in advance; speak to me nearer the time, please.'
'Can't you do that with your friends or family?'	⇨	'I'm feeling a bit overloaded, could you do that with someone else? I still love you.'
'I'm worried about money.'	⇨	'I'm stressed, can you support me?'
'I've got too much work to do so I can't be with you.'	⇨	'Work's busy right now so I can't see you as much. This is temporary and I still love you.'

Communication Skills 101

The key to good communication isn't just down to what we're saying but *how* we say it too. This is where the skill comes in. We can all speak without thinking, generally led by our emotions and not giving any consideration to what it might be like to be on the receiving end of what we're saying. Or we might be so over-focused on the other person and their potential reaction that we are evasive and vague about what we'd like. None of these is very skilled.

As we develop our communication skills, we learn that we can do better at expressing what we want in a way that is constructive.

Avoid 'always', 'never', 'should' and 'must'

These are extreme and likely to evoke defensiveness. There's a big difference between: 'You never listen to me!' and 'When you look at your phone when I'm speaking, it feels like you're not listening. It happens quite a lot.'

Be intentional

Move away from thoughtless interactions to purposeful, considered ways of engaging with your partner and inviting them into important conversations. This often involves us taking time to think before we speak, formulating what we want to express, and choosing the best way of doing so constructively. Phrases to help us are:

- 'What I'd like to get from this conversation is . . .'
- 'There are two specific things I want to share with you, which are . . .'
- 'This is difficult for me to say . . .'
- 'I feel nervous bringing this to you, so please be patient as I explain it.'

Strive to keep conversations healthy

Unless we're paying attention and emotionally regulating, our conversations (and disagreements) can become destructive and unproductive. By noticing this, we can course-correct and bring the discussion back to what we need and what we're trying to achieve.

Phrases to help include:

- 'Please can we slow things down?'
- 'It feels like we're going off track.'
- 'I'm starting to get upset, I think I need a time-out.'
- 'I'm trying to keep my tone of voice calm; please can you do the same?'
- 'What you're saying is important; I want to listen to you. Then can I ask you listen to me?'

Be accountable

Be accountable for what you want to say and take responsibility for yourself and your behaviour. Try not to start sentences with 'you'. When we do, we're in blame territory and our partners can come back with an accusation of their own. Instead, we speak from our own perspective, starting with 'I'. For example, rather than 'You're so bad with money', we can say, 'I'm not comfortable with the amount we're spending when we go out with friends.'

Use gentle language

When we're triggered we are reactive and our communication can be extreme and destructive. We can be in fight mode and the language we use is heightened, exaggerated and meant to do damage. If we are prone to inflammatory language, our work is emotionally regulating and focusing our attention on a gentler approach. When hurt feelings are involved, we need to be especially mindful to be careful with one another. In our reactivity, we forget how fragile our relationships are and how they need to be handled with tenderness and care.

'If it's hysterical, it's historical'

While I'm not a fan of the term 'hysterical', this handy phrase helps remind us to step back and reflect when things are feeling overwhelming or extreme. Often, when we're feeling big feelings or thinking extreme thoughts, we are triggered, which means we are being reminded of a previous hurt or trauma and reacting in the present day with the full force of our fear or rage from the original wound. This is a deeply unconscious process, so a big aspect of our maturing is to recognise when it's happening and bring in loving and compassionate emotional regulation to tend to this deep, and young, pain.

Beware of invalidating

Using language like 'That's not what happened', 'You're being ridiculous' or 'I don't know why you're making such a big deal out of this' are invalidating your partner's feelings and point of view. Our job when our partners are speaking is to listen in an attempt to understand what they want to share with us. Not listening to see where they are wrong. Not listening to correct them. Not listening to decide if their thoughts and feelings are valid. But listening to gain insight into them and what life is like in their shoes. We may not agree, we may not condone what they're saying, we may not even fully get what they're saying, but that doesn't give us the right to invalidate their experience. Instead, we can reframe our attitude to: 'My job is to listen, not form an opinion on what is being said' or 'I want to learn about my partner and I do that by being open to what they tell me.'

Speak how you want to be spoken to

This is a useful reminder for ourselves that we can strive to treat others how we want to be treated, and that includes how we speak to each other. No one's perfect and we'll all have bad moments. However, in terms of our baseline attitude and treatment of others, we can be mindful to afford others the respect and grace we want for ourselves.

Anna and Daryl disagreed on many things. Over the years, their way of communicating had disintegrated into an almost continuous power struggle. Both had a strong need to be right, which meant their focus was on proving the other very wrong. It was so normalised that neither felt it was a problem until their eldest daughter started being hostile to them and her grandparents. Daryl's brother pointed out that their daughter had probably learnt this from Daryl's argumentativeness and sharp tongue.

Shocked, Daryl applied himself and learnt the difference between aggressive and assertive, and realised a lot of his communication was disrespectful and not a good example to his daughter. Both he and Anna took responsibility for their communication clangers and started being more intentional in how they spoke to each other.

Affectionate language for the avoidantly attached

Individuals with avoidant attachment tendencies aren't always naturally affectionate, either physically or verbally. However, to maintain the warmth and intimacy in our relationships, it's useful to stretch ourselves in achievable ways so we can be more expressive to our loved ones. Phrases that are not over-the-top or seemingly insincere include:

- 'I know I don't say it enough, but you mean the world to me.'
- 'You're very attractive to me.'
- 'I like being with you.'
- 'I think you're _____ [sexy, strong, accomplished].'
- 'I care about you.'
- 'My life is better with you in it.'
- 'I love you.'

Likewise, these individuals may cringe being on the receiving end of overt verbal affection. We can let them know they are cared for, admired and found attractive in simple ways, such as:

- 'Someone's looking good today.'
- 'That was a hilarious remark.'
- 'I am here for you.'
- 'That was a very impressive achievement.'
- 'We're a good team.'
- 'I love you.'

To be totally safe, ask your partner what they would consider huge compliments - and then you'll know for sure.

Apologise rather than explain

It seems many of us have negative associations with apologising. Perhaps apologising is symbolic to us: it means we are wrong, we have failed, we committed an offence or we are weak. All of these things are unacceptable to us, so we don't apologise. And if we didn't mean to hurt or cause offense, it's even more important we don't apologise – *because we haven't done anything wrong.*

While this makes sense on the face of it, it's not relational. When we say we've not done anything wrong we are talking from our own perspective. We are disregarding our partners' perspective or experience.

We're also basing our thoughts on our intention. If we didn't intend to hurt anyone, and don't believe anything we did or said was hurtful, we will inadvertently invalidate our partners by explaining that to them. In other words, the message is: 'What *I* think about your feelings is more important than your feelings. Let me tell you what you should be feeling.' Not a good look!

By apologising, we aren't admitting to being a bad person or to being wrong, and it certainly is not weak. Apologising is a social skill which communicates: 'I care about how you feel. If I hurt you – even unintentionally – I care. And I'm sorry. I don't want to hurt you.'

We can overthink it and put too much negative association on apologising. Instead, we can focus our attention on developing the self-esteem we need to apologise because someone we care about was hurt by something we said or did. We can hold our hands up that our behaviour was not so great, rather than that we are not-so-great people. There's a difference.

How to Make a Repair

We're all human and will sometimes behave in less than stellar ways. Then, it's how we make repairs that will influence our relationship's ability to go the distance or not. There are many bumps in the road when we're doing life together and it's important to keep the relationship in the best condition possible for the journey, and that means regular repairs.

A way to remember how to repair is to VALUE the relationship:

V – VALIDATE YOUR PARTNER

This is the hardest step! Even if we don't agree or understand, we must be careful to not invalidate our partners. Hear what they're saying and let them know you care by validating their experience. Often this is 75 per cent of the repair, so don't downplay its importance. Good phrases to use are: 'I can see why that would be upsetting', 'That makes sense', 'I get what you're saying.'

A – BEGIN PREPARING TO APOLOGISE

It can take time for us to be ready and able to do so genuinely. Listening to your partner, and practising empathy and compassion, will help you become willing to apologise.

L – LEAN IN TO THE DISCOMFORT

These conversations are often difficult – expect that and work your resilience muscle. Defensiveness is often our first reaction, which protects us from the more nuanced feelings we might have, such as regret, embarrassment or confusion. Tolerate this discomfort and be there for your partner.

U – TRY TO UNDERSTAND

We have a deep need to be understood by the people we love. As your partner talks to you and communicates their thoughts, try to see things from their point of view and use it as an opportunity to deepen your understanding of them.

E – EXPRESS YOUR APOLOGY LOVINGLY

This is the last step for a reason. By this stage, we have given ourselves time to calm down, hear our partners, lean in this new behaviour, and become willing to own our part in things and apologise. A lot of the work has already been done as your partner will hopefully feel acknowledged, heard and understood by your efforts from the previous steps.

Good apologies sound like:

- 'I apologise for being insensitive to your feelings.'
- 'I am sorry for my poor choice of words and for disrespecting you.'
- 'I was wrong. I apologise.'
- 'I really regret my outburst. I am truly sorry for not controlling my anger.'
- 'That was not my finest moment. I am sorry for _____ '

Add detail to show you understand what you're apologising for. Keep your face open, your language calm and gentle, and your attitude reconciliatory.

> ## WAIT
>
> We can often fall into overexplaining, ranting or saying things that are not relevant or constructive. When we complain, we can go on and on about subjects, go off on tangents or vent uncontrollably. It is completely natural and healthy to talk and work things out with our partners; however, if we know we can go overboard (without a clear objective or any particular outcome in mind), we would do well to remind ourselves to WAIT and ask ourselves: **why am I talking**? Only proceed when we can answer that question and know our aim.

How to Do Things Differently During Arguments

Changing your unhelpful behaviours when you're in an argument is transformative. It's a great way to start challenging your patterns and changing your unhelpful behaviour, like reactivity.

1. **Recognise when you're triggered and dysregulated.** How does it feel in your body? Heart racing, tense? This shows your anger/anxiety has been triggered and can give you a warning to take care.

2. **You will start thinking extreme, damaging, negative thoughts** which shift you from normal interaction into fight, flight, freeze or fawn responses. Any perceived threat will be responded to in this primitive way. Your body and brain are getting ready to fight. Often, we don't realise when this is happening. Are you able to listen? Do you have empathy for your partner?

Can you be compassionate? If the answer is no, you are triggered. Know yourself well enough to recognise when it's happening so you can do something different.

3. **Pause.** When you notice you're triggered, start pausing internally. Reactivity is when there's no pause. You're in fight mode. Pause is where your power lives.

4. **Stay in control of yourself, your behaviour and what you're saying.** Do some breathwork and emotional regulation exercises (see Chapter 7). Do not respond to your partner until you've paused and given thought to what you want to say. Remember your personal boundaries.

5. **State your needs.** 'Let's slow things down', 'Can we be kind to each other?', 'Please hold my hand.' This calms and regulates the system and encourages co-regulation.

6. **Remember your goal.** When we're triggered it becomes about survival and we forget our bigger purpose: to be a loving, kind partner. It might feel good to lash out but in terms of your goal, it won't help you get where you want to go.

We can be accountable. We are responsible for our behaviour. When we're arguing and emotionally dysregulated we have lost control and we need to do whatever is necessary to get back in control, so we can return to a place of love.

Being able to keep our reactions, tone of voice, behaviour and thinking constructive prevents disagreements or misunderstandings from escalating or becoming damaging. This can sometimes be very tough to do when we're having difficult conversations.

In those moments, it helps to know of ways you can look after yourself by staying calm and regulating your emotions.

Experiment with ways of emotionally regulating to find those that work for you, as they can avert disaster in these situations.

Dignity checking

Try this exercise: Think of three conversations when you felt embarrassed by your behaviour, ashamed and/or did not achieve anything constructive or useful.

Now think of three instances when you communicated well. You felt proud of yourself, you were composed, you got your point across and you spoke confidently.

Analyse these exchanges in these terms: your emotional state, the time and place of the communication, your clarity on what you wanted to say, your tone of voice and language, and your level of respect for the other person and yourself.

You can then explore how you might have done things differently with a bit more intentionality, so these damaging interactions do not continue.

Schedule a relationship meeting

It's helpful to approach the communication in our relationships with a level of organisation and efficiency. Having a regular relationship meeting – every week or fortnight – is a good way of achieving that. Often, there is not a predetermined time and place to discuss our relationship issues, and we can fall into the habit of complaining, ruminating or nitpicking instead, not resolving anything and creating a negative atmosphere in the relationship.

A small amount of time put aside for a relationship meeting creates the space required. Any issues can be brought to this meeting, as well as it being an opportunity to practise gratitude and appreciation.

A suggested relationship meeting agenda might be:

- **Begin with appreciation.** Start the meeting by highlighting all the positives that have taken place since the previous meeting. This is an opportunity to tune in to things your partner has said or done that you appreciated and are grateful for. For example: 'I appreciated you visiting my mother with me' or 'I'm really grateful for your calm when the kids are playing up.' You can sneak in some compliments or validation here too.
- **Go through your diaries.** You can look at the weeks ahead and what is taking place, your responsibilities and social obligations. This is an opportunity for you to share your expectations with your partner, what you would like from them and how you'd like your obligations to be fulfilled. Your partner can then do the same. This troubleshoots disappointment and goes against the unhelpful thinking styles of mind reading and fortune telling (see page 189).
- **Goal-setting and review.** The next portion of the agenda reviews the areas for growth in the relationship and goals you have set/requested. You can make further requests of one another and review what you are both working on. For example: 'Last time, I asked you to be aware of your tone of voice when irritated and I've seen you rein yourself in recently. Thank you. Please keep that up. And can I ask you now to give me more compliments? I'd love one a day!'
- **Agree the date and time of the next meeting.**
- **Finish with gratitude.** The meeting can come to a close by doing a gratitude list about the aspects of your partner and your relationship that are good, positive, inspiring and joyful. For example: 'I love and am grateful for your smile when I do something silly' or 'I'm grateful for your commitment to these meetings' or 'I love your gorgeous body.'

- **After-meeting contact.** This would be a great moment to do the heart hug breathing exercise on page 177 or finish with an embrace or even sex.

This agenda can be amended and adapted to what works for you and your partner, and can be updated as things progress and your needs change.

Practice makes perfect. Communication skills can be practised all day every day, and the more we experiment with what works for us, the more we will see our interactions become calmer and more mature.

In the next chapter, we will explore boundaries in the context of our intimate relationships and how we can keep ourselves emotionally safe without going into our insecurely attached defences and unhelpful coping strategies.

Journalling prompts

- Do you experience challenges with communicating constructively? What examples can you think of where you communicated in ineffective ways?
- Can you recognise any of the passive, aggressive or assertive behaviours?
- What non-verbal ways of communicating do you do that aren't helpful?
- Which communication clangers are present in your relationship and what has been the consequence of them?
- What alternatives or tools would you like to practise?

CHAPTER 10

Living a Boundaried Life

A big part of creating safety is having boundaries – around how much we give, how much we do, who we allow into our life, and how extreme we allow ourselves to get.

When we're insecurely attached and triggered, we don't have any boundaries. Our fear is in charge and we've lost control of our thinking and behaving. It's all too easy for us to focus on the people around us and how they are 'causing' the 'problems'. We become resentful and can even be a bit superior. The focus becomes how to control others into behaving how we want them to, rather than taking responsibility for our emotions and reactions, and how we are volunteering ourselves to any unhealthy interactions.

Or we feel so weak and inconsequential that we blame ourselves for every little thing and allow ourselves to get swept along with whatever the latest drama may be. We feel persecuted by the other person, trapped and unable to do anything about it. We believe that, unless they change, nothing will change. We are embroiled, enmeshed and exhausted.

How to tell if boundaries are lacking in your relationship

- You feel too nervous to speak to your partner about important stuff.
- You feel taken for granted and/or compromised.
- There is no resolution to your arguing.
- You've stopped asking things of each other.
- You feel trapped and unable to do anything about it.
- You frequently lose your temper.
- You feel guilty or resentful a lot of the time.
- The relationship is not equal.
- The relationship is high-conflict, dramatic or addictive.
- The relationship is false and pretend-nice.

Having boundaries is imperative – they help us stay safe and dignified. However, boundaries are often misunderstood. Are they walls that keep people out? No. Does it entail being mean to people? Definitely not. Simply, boundaries are what we use to keep relationships appropriate, healthy and thriving. They guide us to what is healthy and what is too extreme. What is caring and what is too compromising or enabling. What is supportive and what is disempowering (for other people and us). What makes us feel good or what makes us feel drained or manipulated. What is our responsibility and what is someone else's responsibility.

And they also teach the people around us what our limits are, how to care for us and what is on offer with us.

What are boundaries for?

- Boundaries are about maintaining our well-being: managing anxiety, overwhelm and our triggers.
- Emotional boundaries are about helping us to be in control of how extreme we get, mentally and emotionally.
- Relational boundaries help us stay close to people but distanced from dysfunction.

Five Steps to Setting Healthy Limits and Boundaries

Step 1: Assess the person or situation and take responsibility

A common boundary problem is disowning our choices and trying to lay the responsibility for them on someone else. Think for a moment how often you use the phrases 'I had to', 'They made me' or 'Well, someone had to' when explaining why you did or did not do something.

From a mental health perspective, we want to strive for emotional stability and mental resilience, so it's useful and important to be reviewing our reactions to certain people and situations all the time. This simply means being aware of how much energy they require from us so we can become better at managing our energy reserves as we go about our lives.

Often, it's our bodies that are the most reliable judges of that. Certain people or circumstances may bring up anxiety (we notice we hold our breath, our heart races or we begin to dread and think negatively), fear (our nerves start fizzing, we sweat or get the chills) or shame (hot and cold rushes, tingling sensations in our body). This is key information to have to begin looking after ourselves, we can figure out what boundaries will be useful to put in place so we don't get triggered.

Some questions to ask yourself:

- Is my partner open to discussing boundaries? Is it appropriate in this situation?
- Is it necessary to verbalise the boundaries to the other person or simply implement them in my own behaviour and thinking?
- What is realistic to expect of this person or situation? (Managing expectations.)
- How can I look after myself and take responsibility for how available I make myself?
- How can I have internal boundaries about how much emotion and time I allow this situation to take from me? (See Step 3.)
- How can I be kind and respectful but still do what I need to do to look after myself (which is my responsibility)?

Step 2: Calmly speak up for yourself and express what you need

Having boundaries is the opposite of being passive or aggressive. Rather than not saying anything, or saying things abrasively, learning to speak up for ourselves helps us to develop composure in our lives and relationships.

We can get into very bad habits in our relationships, but through reminding ourselves of the respect that is the foundation for our intimate partnerships, we can learn to express our needs with dignity. It's therefore so important to notice if you are likely to be reactive so you can breathe, emotionally regulate and regain full control of yourself. Then, share with your partner, talking about yourself (start your sentences with 'I') and not them. For example:

- 'I'm worrying about the housework. Can we make a list of what needs to be done and share the chores?'
- 'I need to pause this conversation, I'm feeling overwhelmed.'
- 'I need to think about that; can we speak about this tomorrow?'
- 'In future, please ask me before making decisions that involve me.'
- 'I'm feeling hurt about our lack of affection and intimacy.'
- 'I would like to make time to discuss our spending and finances.'

Step 3: Implement internal boundaries

For those of us with anxiety, depression or attachment issues, it isn't just things outside of us we need to protect ourselves from – it's things on the inside too; things like extreme negative thinking, unhealthy beliefs and uncontrollable emotions. Without boundaries around these things, we are likely to stay very unwell and can cause ourselves and others a lot of suffering.

When we are triggered into our anxiety or avoidance, we will experience the familiar pain of bitterness, sadness, disappointment or worry. And we will feel the anxiety, anger and hurt that go with them. This can be a rollercoaster ride we really do not need to go on.

Implementing internal boundaries helps us stay steady; they calm and reassure us so we can move away from the extremes and back into balance.

Examples of internal boundaries

- Not using abusive language in your head to describe yourself or others.
- Observing when your thoughts are extreme, rigid and inflexible, and bringing them back to moderation.
- Noticing automatic negative thoughts (ANTs) and resisting cynicism and bitterness. Remind yourself thoughts aren't facts.
- Recognising when you're triggered and taking a time-out.
- Having distractions and activities at hand to help shift repetitive thoughts.
- Using supportive self-talk to shift your perspective:
  o 'I am strong and can get through this.'
  o 'I am allowed to feel peace.'
  o 'My responsibility is first to myself and keeping my thinking constructive.'
  o 'It's okay to feel angry, and I can express it appropriately.'

Step 4: Recognise that you let a lot of basics slide: respect, care, manners and kindness

It's often in our most intimate relationships that we are the most boundaryless. In our hurt or anger, we feel justified to let our frustrations out on our partners with the full force of our fear, rage and upset. However, in these instances, we are not in control of ourselves. This is the 'fight' in our trauma response (see page 49) and it can become normalised – and destructive – very quickly.

Sometimes, we are fighting with our partners to draw them close and to prove their passion for us. Other times, we are fighting to push our partners away to create the space and distance we need. Whatever the unconscious motivation, fight mode is not going to meet our needs or create the safety our nervous systems need. It will do the opposite.

Commit to speaking and behaving in ways that respect you and the other person. Notice when you're triggered, observing your tone of voice, language and attitude. Practise self-care: self-soothe, emotionally regulate, communicate with care and patience, and stay adult. Again, talk from the 'I' and not the 'you', and be as specific as you can:

- 'I would love some help with ____.'
- 'I'd appreciate you just listening to me; I'm not ready for solutions yet.'
- 'I really enjoy spending time together – let's plan a fun day this weekend.'
- 'I need some downtime on my own – let's meet up later tonight.'
- 'I'm so sorry you are going through a tough time.'
- 'I'm feeling too angry to continue this discussion. Let's talk after dinner.'

Step 5: Live your life in a boundaried way

As we practise speaking up for ourselves, having limits and developing internal boundaries, we will discover the enormous benefit of boundaries. They can become part of our lives and keep us well: they increase and maintain our self-esteem as we demonstrate our self-worth on a daily basis; they keep our partnerships alive and awake and accountable, and they stretch us to keep growing, embodying and meeting our ever-changing wants and needs.

Previous chapters have shown that we have the capacity to pause and question whether something is right for us before saying yes. We know it is not someone else's job to look after us – it's our job. We make sure we are *choosing* what and who we have in our lives, and embrace them wholeheartedly. It's a great way to live.

Living a boundaried life is a mindset. We deeply feel our responsibility to ourselves and having our own back. And we take it seriously.

What healthy boundaries facilitate

- Saying no without guilt.
- Asking for what you want or need.
- Taking care of yourself.
- Behaving according to your own values.
- Feeling safe expressing difficult emotions.
- Being treated as an equal.
- Being in tune with your feelings.
- Taking responsibility for your own happiness.

How to maintain boundaries

Here are basic but important factors to address when thinking about maintaining boundaries:

1: Stress

If you are experiencing stress, either in your personal life or at work, your insecure symptoms can worsen. We may struggle to stay adult or keep conversations constructive and kind. Our avoidance or anxiety will kick in as a way of coping. We can become emotionally depleted and have little left to bring to the relationship, or the relationship becomes the dumping ground for our frustrations. Self-care is imperative to keep us responsible to both ourselves and our partners (see page 158).

2: Alcohol and drugs

I know this is obvious, but drinking or drugging to excess, or arguing when under the influence, is highly unhelpful. Likewise, when hung-over. Notice if this is becoming a problem in itself. Drug use impairs us neurologically and physiologically, leaving us susceptible to mood changes, irritability, shutting down or thinking the worst. Lifestyle changes are often required in these areas if we are experiencing difficulty in our relationships.

3: Numbing-out online activity

It's difficult to be relational if much of our time and headspace is spent on solitary, mood-altering activities online. This impacts the brain and shuts down emotional, social and sexual impulses.

4: Hormones

If I had my way, everyone would regularly have their hormones checked, regardless of age. Book in to see your doctor to check hormones such as oestrogen, progesterone, testosterone or thyroid hormones. These can play large, and often unacknowledged or invisible, roles in our emotional, sexual and relational well-being.

5: Peer or family pressure

Consider the outside influences you have in your life. Do your family and friends feed into unhelpful narratives about relationships and people? Or are they supportive and encouraging? Friends and family can have a huge impact on how we view our relationship, and sometimes their attitudes and philosophies will be rooted in their own issues and insecurities. Listen to people who've done the work and are having the kind of relationships you want.

Sipho had stressed about money most of his life and, now that he was in a long-term relationship, his stress had become all-consuming. He was in a good, stable job and earned a fair salary, but he still worried about providing for his partner and their life together. He didn't share this with his partner, however, instead lying awake at night, fretting and ruminating about his latest credit card bill. His partner seemed to have no problem with spending large amounts on their home and socialising, which Sipho felt was completely unnecessary.

Finally, when Sipho's emotional health threatened to derail either his job or his relationship, he spoke to his partner and, after an initial bit of tension, they were able to work on a realistic budget and negotiate some boundaries around their spending. To his surprise, Sipho's partner liked sharing the responsibility with him and the exercise brought them closer together.

A Word on Consistency

Secure attachment relies on consistency. Of course, none of us can be anything near perfectly consistent all the time. However, we can appreciate its importance and prioritise it. When we or our partners are erratic or unpredictable, or predictably chaotic or closed off, secure attachment cannot happen. Boundaries are about helping us to avoid the extremes in how we behave and keeping certain secure-making ways of relating consistent the majority of the time: respectfulness, patience, playfulness, relative calm and an optimistic attitude. They help us to reduce self-defeating ways of behaving that are rooted in inconsistency and fear.

Individuals with anxiously attached tendencies can struggle to manage their emotions and need to consistently bring more moderation to relationships; **individuals with avoidantly attached tendencies** can struggle to be consistently present in the relationship and need to bring in more relationship participation.

Both would do well to devote their attention to this aspect of security. Consistency is crucial.

What boundaries teach us

- We understand that the language we use in our own heads and when speaking with other people really matters. Being respectful and patient increases our self-esteem; being disrespectful and snide decreases our self-esteem.
- We listen to our bodies and what they communicate to us all the time. We tune in to what and who

provokes anxiety and stress, and also what and who evokes calm and safety. This serves as a compass for us and we make our choices based on what and who feels right.

- We say what we mean and mean what we say. No more walking on eggshells, no more people-pleasing - just polite, respectful honesty as we state our needs and make requests. We are who we are and we let others be who they are.

Ask for What You Want

Does this sound like an over-simplification? Maybe. But this is the best boundary to ward off disappointment. In so many cases in our partnerships, we are distressed by our partners not doing what we want, without us ever having made it explicit. We think, 'If they really loved me, they would know what I want' or 'It's so obvious.' Boundaries invite us to take responsibility for what we want, and we do this by taking action to make it happen. If you would really love white tulips for your birthday, tell your partner, 'I would love it if you could get me white tulips for my birthday.' If you want to leave early for the long drive, say the exact time you'd like to leave. If you want pasta for dinner, say you want pasta.

What can happen instead is we tell our partners afterwards, when we're disappointed or annoyed. 'Why couldn't you have just bought me some lovely flowers?' we lament tearfully. Or, 'I knew we'd be late – again!' we declare angrily. Or, 'Have you ever noticed we always have what *you* want for dinner?' we ask with chagrin.

A brilliant habit to develop is asking, asking, asking. Will your life become constant asking and requesting from your partner? Kind of. But it also liberates us from the victim position, in which we are perennially discouraged and left feeling let down. It's our responsibility to speak up in our relationships and it's important to keep our voice strong in our partnerships.

This isn't an opportunity to become a demanding despot, but it is an opportunity for people to meet your needs, and for you and your partner to learn what it is you really like, and vice versa.

Our expectations can be unconscious until they are unmet

Sometimes, the hardest aspect of this exercise is getting clear on what we want ahead of time ourselves. We may not consciously think about or consider what would be best, only registering later when our expectations have been undercut.

Many of us don't know what our wants and needs are. But that doesn't stop us getting furious when our partners don't either!

The first step, therefore, is getting clarity on what it is we want from our partners – what matters to us. This can be revealed by the same arguments you keep having, what irks you, and what causes particular relationship dissatisfaction for you.

How we communicate our requests is important too. Unboundaried throwaway remarks or angry proclamations are going to be received by the recipient as 'moaning' and either evoke defensiveness or not be taken seriously. Requests can be made calmly, in a non-accusatory and neutral way, looking at each other, with an agreement at the end, whether that's a head nod or further discussion (see the assertiveness section in Chapter 9 for more inspiration).

Ways to ask for what you want

Request Examples:

- 'Please can we agree we will text at least once a day?'
- 'I'd like to keep Thursday nights free just for us.'
- 'Could you fold the laundry while I mop the floor?'
- 'Let's agree when we start raising our voices in a disagreement, we will stop the conversation.'
- 'I'd love it if you could cook dinner tomorrow night.'
- 'I'd like us to check with one another before we spend more than ___ from the joint account.'
- 'I want to connect with you physically: let's have sex later.'
- 'Please don't gossip about me with your family. I'm open to hearing your concerns directly.'
- 'I'm feeling nervous about a work meeting; could you big me up a bit?'
- 'When we go out on Saturday, I don't want us to get drunk; shall we have a drink limit and agree a time we'll leave?'
- 'I'm having a tough time at the moment. Could you hold me?'

Of course, a big caveat is: what if they don't do what we want despite us asking? We may have told our partners a thousand times and yet the behaviour remains lacking. The answer is: we keep asking.

The human brain requires huge amounts of repetition before an idea takes root. And if something doesn't come naturally to us, it takes even more repetition before a new behaviour or change takes place. Our relationships require input from us – we need to have a voice; this is what keeps our partnerships growing and healthy.

If, after an extended period of time, the change you want is not happening, go back to the emotional regulation technique: 'change, accept, let go' (see page 171). After trying to change it, our options are to accept the status quo and accept our partners for who they are – certain aspects of our partners and relationships won't change and so we spend some time getting okay with that. Our partners aren't problems to be fixed, and often we need to work our acceptance muscle and let things be. That's part of letting go – to let go of the desired behaviour change, to let go of our angst and upset about it, to not let it get under our skin . . .

However, if none of that is possible, we may have to think about letting go of the relationship entirely. It's not fair to stay with someone we can't fundamentally accept or who won't change – at all – for the betterment of the relationship. (We'll cover this in much more detail at the end of Chapter 14.)

Desensitise to your fear of rejection – an unusual approach

An unconventional, but effective REBT tool to help us overcome a fear of rejection is called shame-attacking. It involves exposing ourselves to our greatest fears, repeatedly and on purpose. This helps us challenge our fears (what might *actually* happen if we are rejected, for example? Will we collapse, keel over, faint?) and desensitise to these aspects of life that are unfortunate, but occur frequently. By proactively seeking out or creating rejecting scenarios we put ourselves in the driver's seat and discover that although it may be uncomfortable or sad or bruising, we can survive rejection. By attacking our fear and the shame that surrounds it, we discover we can become more robust and handle difficult emotions.

A course of shame-attacking to reduce our fear of rejection could involve creating a rejecting situation every day for one month. This could include: calling your local restaurant and asking for a free meal; asking the bus driver if you can drive the bus; approaching random people and saying, 'Are you looking for me?'; asking someone you don't know at the coffee shop if you can have a sip of their coffee, or asking for a discount when purchasing anything.

You will hear 'no' and you will be rejected. After a while, the notion of rejection will lose its power as you realise it happens often and it isn't (and needn't be) so crushing. We can tolerate it and, in the context of a relationship, our self-esteem can remain intact. A seemingly strange approach, however it can be very impactful!

Shifting Away from Over-Functioning

There are many reasons for over-functioning, most of them complicated and also very sad. Being kind, caring and giving are wonderful traits, but that's not what over-functioning is about. As the name suggests, over-functioning is when we cross boundaries and do too much, taking responsibility for things beyond our control, overextending ourselves both personally and professionally, and contorting ourselves in an attempt to make our relationships work.

What might the fears be that drive your over-functioning? Maybe you fear you won't be as liked by others if you do less. Maybe you equate your self-worth with doing for others. Maybe you have a need to be needed. Maybe you are scared what will happen if you aren't managing it all. What might you see in your relationship? Will you see how little is on offer (which you mask with your over-functioning)?

There's solace in over-functioning. With so much of life and people outside of our control, our incessant doing gives us a false sense of *doing something* about our challenging lives and loves. But our over-functioning rarely achieves anything other than the perpetuation of our patterns and the role we play in relationships. In its extreme, we can burn out and become very unwell.

Boundaries for over-functioners

Look at your to-do list and highlight the following:

- tasks that are your responsibility
- tasks that are other people's responsibility
- tasks you've been asked to do
- tasks you've not been asked to do but want/plan to do anyway

Having done that:

- Assign the tasks that are not your responsibility to the appropriate person, or simply give yourself permission to not do them (you may need the emotional regulation skills in Chapter 7 for this).

- Question the wisdom/benefit of doing what no one has asked you to do.
- Look at the list as a whole and ask yourself what you can realistically do (giving time for rest, for play and for yourself).
- Go over the list and highlight at least five points to delegate to others.

In work and family meetings, practise the STOP technique (page 167) and stay silent when something needs to be done, **pause** and let others volunteer. Don't fill the silence.

You can also do the following:

- Use your breathing and communication exercises and speak up if you are doing other people's work.
- Make a request every day for your partner, family, friends or colleagues to do something you would have automatically done.
- Read and reread this book to focus your time and energy on worthwhile tasks that will help you develop your self-esteem, assertiveness and relational skills.
- Schedule at least three things every week that are just for you, that help you to relax, replenish and enjoy yourself.

Show me people happy in their relationship and I will show you people who are open with each other, respectful and really care about each other's experience. They look after themselves as well as each other. In short, they live a boundaried life, with love, not fear, at its centre.

Journalling prompts

- How can you tell boundaries are lacking in your relationship?
- Why do you think boundaries are important? Give examples of poor boundaries you've experienced.
- How might you incorporate the five steps to setting healthy limits and boundaries into your life? Consider your relationship, but also work, friends and family.
- Think of five requests you could make that would help your relationship and home life.
- In what ways do you over-function and want to challenge that?

PART IV

Solutions: Confronting Relationship Traps

Adult attachment is complicated enough, but it becomes even more complicated when we are in relationships and have to navigate the attachment styles of everyone involved. We are all familiar with this discomfort and difficulty.

There are multiple layers of complexity when our attachment systems come together with other people's, and everyone's stories, expectations and fears play out in glorious Technicolor. There's a huge amount that can (and does) go wrong, so many traps that we can fall into, and so much unconscious behaviour that goes unexamined and unaddressed.

Let's look at some relational dynamics, how they inevitably play out and impact the relationship, and how we might bring a more securely attached way of relating into the mix.

CHAPTER 11

The Anxious Avoidant Dance

When predominantly anxious and avoidantly attached individuals meet, they have the capacity to really excite one another because of their contrasting relating styles, which creates a lot of tension and excitement in the early phase of relationships. The person who leans towards avoidant attachment allows themselves to get closer than they normally would, and the person who can be anxiously attached revels in the attention. There can often be a strong sexual connection which adds to the passion and intoxicating nature of this relationship at the beginning.

After a period of time, however, their nervous systems will go back to their familiar ways of relating. The anxiously attached person will continue to want (or will want more) attention and reassurance from their partner, while the avoidantly attached person will begin requiring some space and autonomy.

The avoidantly attached person will need to step away and, depending on how extreme the situation is, they may end the relationship or simply need to withdraw for a period of time. The anxiously attached person will get triggered into their abandonment fears, which will provoke them to pursue their partners for more closeness. This will trigger the avoidantly attached person's smothering fears and they will retreat further into withdrawal and shutdown. This is then often repeated – the anxiously attached wanting more and stepping into the relationship, and the avoidantly attached wanting less and stepping away from the relationship.

Eventually, the person who by now will be very anxiously attached will become so disillusioned they will move into ambivalence and retreat from the relationship. The avoidantly attached will notice this change and will begin to fear losing them. They then resume engaging in the relationship, giving the attention the anxiously attached has craved so much. The partnership returns back to the start of the cycle, where they enjoy a period of connection, sex and feeling special . . . until attachment fears come to the fore and the cycle then plays out again.

The more this is repeated, the more it is reinforced and imprinted in our nervous systems.

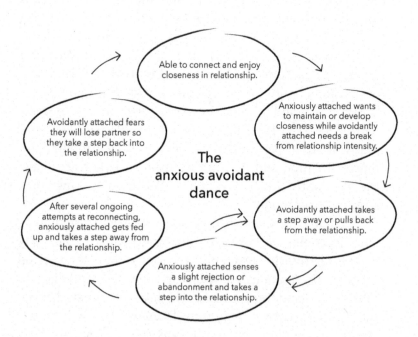

The anxious avoidant dance

Able to connect and enjoy closeness in relationship.

Anxiously attached wants to maintain or develop closeness while avoidantly attached needs a break from relationship intensity.

Avoidantly attached takes a step away or pulls back from the relationship.

Anxiously attached senses a slight rejection or abandonment and takes a step into the relationship.

After several ongoing attempts at reconnecting, anxiously attached gets fed up and takes a step away from the relationship.

Avoidantly attached fears they will lose partner so they take a step back into the relationship.

Anyone who has experience of this dance knows how excruciating it is. By breaking it down and analysing what is going on for each other and the people involved, we can bring compassion to this process. Both are suffering in their own ways and both are playing out their familiar and (painfully) complementary ways of attaching.

This dynamic accounts for the majority of insecure partnerships. But finding a way through is possible if those involved are willing to grow and adapt.

Below are many of the challenges these relationships face. Some or all may ring true for you and your experience. We'll explore each one in detail and look at what needs to be worked on for these partnerships to become more secure and equal.

Challenges for anxious and avoidant relationships

- The needs of the other person trigger a trauma response.
- Needs of the people involved conflict.
- There are negative beliefs about the other person's behaviour.
- Both lose control of thinking and feeling (anxious – escalates; avoidant – withdraws).
- Everyone involved has a low distress tolerance.
- Partners easily become emotionally dysregulated (anxious – externalising; avoidant – internalising or shutting down).
- Relationships are viewed in a negative way (anxious – unfulfilling and painful; avoidant – overwhelming and frustrating).
- One or both partners struggle with empathy and compassion.

The needs of the other person trigger a trauma response

For people in this dynamic, it can be difficult to appreciate that the other person is suffering too. The truth is that attachment wounding is playing out painfully for all involved, so it's important to bring compassion to one another. It's tragic that our insecure needs trigger our partners' trauma response. However, if we are anxiously attached, we can understand that once our anxiety has taken over and our need to connect has become all-consuming, this will overwhelm the avoidantly attached person (who values us enough and wants us enough to be in a relationship with us but struggles with ongoing connectivity). Likewise, we can also understand that, if we are avoidantly attached, when we disengage from the relationship to focus on our own autonomy needs this will alarm and signal abandonment to the anxiously attached person, who seeks solace in connection and proximity.

A key takeaway learning is that our partners are not trying to thwart our needs or make our lives a misery, but rather are simply operating from the relational adaptations that provided their way of feeling safe in relationships.

This relationship *can* offer the opportunity to heal their and our attachment wounds and create more security for everyone involved, with love, effort and care.

HOW TO BREAK THE PATTERN

Emotional regulation is crucial to ward against being frequently triggered into trauma response. We can recognise the specific thinking and behaviour we fall back on when we are anxious or avoidant and use skills to help us not act on them or to rein them in. We can understand and have compassion for the trauma wounding it is touching in us. This might apply to a person with anxiety, who can realise some of their thoughts are extreme or catastrophising and need to be right-sized, or a person with avoidance, who realises dismissive thoughts or opinions of their partner are a defence and a distortion, and are not to be believed. Develop emotional regulation skills every day and recognise distorted thinking (see chapters 7 and 8).

Needs of the people involved conflict

It's very human for us to reject that which we don't understand. And the fact that our partners have such different needs to our own puts us in danger of rejecting their needs or over-focusing on our own.

Not only are their needs different to our needs, they are in direct conflict. When a partner wants closeness and another partner wants space, this can be hugely disconnecting. Likewise, when we want some breathing room and our partners are seemingly all over us, that is very trying too. These conflicting needs can become representations of complete incompatibility or, if everyone involved is willing to work on themselves, they can become managed in a loving relationship, whereby awareness and kindness help our needs to be met and wounds to be healed.

HOW TO BREAK THE PATTERN

Work on accepting that the other person has conflicting needs. A lot of our efforts go into resisting and rejecting our partners' needs because they are so different to our own. Being relational means respecting one another and trying to do what is best for the relationship, which in this instance would be moving away from who's right and who's wrong to more acceptance and negotiation. Acceptance can be very challenging. Say to yourself, 'I can let my partner be who they are. I accept them for who they are.' Thereafter, use emotional regulation skills if necessary (see Chapter 7) and have a relationship meeting about how both your needs could be reasonably acknowledged or addressed (see page 232).

There are negative beliefs about the other person's behaviour

Both of these attachment styles possess negative thinking and beliefs about relationships and other people. The anxiously attached person can experience avoidant behaviour as deeply cruel; the person with avoidant attachment can experience anxious behaviour as stifling and suffocating. When this becomes part of the relationship landscape, we can begin to think very negative things about our partners and their behaviour. This is a key aspect of what maintains the dance, and our insecure attachment. We feel hurt by the other person, keep ourselves in the victim position, and do not proactively do anything constructive. Because we can feel (and be) traumatised by these insecure ways of relating, part of our 'fight' response is we can make our partners the enemy and turn our relationships into a battleground. In this way, we ensure our unhappiness and so our pattern continues.

HOW TO BREAK THE PATTERN

Catch negative thoughts and beliefs about the other person and reframe them towards appreciation and respect. This is about changing the atmosphere of the relationship. Often, tension and dissatisfaction permeate our romantic environments, and instead of being relaxed and loving, we are primed for the next wrong move our partners will inevitably make. This is part of the dance and is very important to disrupt. We need to take responsibility for our thoughts and attitude and commit to keeping our interactions constructive and our tone kind (see chapters 8 and 9 on distorted thinking and healthy communication). Effort can be made every day to express something we appreciate about our partners, and to be mindful to maintain respect for each other.

Both lose control of thinking and feeling

In our anxiety, we will lose control of our emotions and how we express ourselves; we become hugely negative and catastrophise, and we can be impulsive and compulsive (messaging too much, monitoring and intruding, stalking online, gossiping with friends and negatively spiralling). In our avoidance, we will lose control of our thinking and how we view our partners, which can become hugely negative and sometimes superior, and we can be shut-down or rude (saying unpleasant things/being blunt, stonewalling, retreating into numbing-out activities, moaning to friends and negatively spiralling).

When our trauma wounding has been activated, our prefrontal cortex – the part of the brain in charge of empathy – shuts down. We become hugely preoccupied with ourselves and, in this way, we are not relational. It's important we recognise that we have lost control of our thoughts and behaviour. Even though it may not feel so dramatic, it still does not mean we are in control. Especially when we are in an avoidant process, we can feel overly in control, which we like. However, that simply means our need for control is out of control.

HOW TO BREAK THE PATTERN

Take responsibility for reactions, and stay in control of thoughts and behaviour. A big trap of this partnership is falling into blame. Because we're hurt, we can abdicate responsibility and resentfully blame our partners and their flaws and failings. We can lack boundaries and lash out at each other, descend into dark and destructive thought processes and let our negative thinking and emotions run the show. There will be legitimate concerns and issues the relationship needs to address; however, that will not happen until we can take responsibility for ourselves and keep ourselves regulated and in control (see Chapter 10 for boundary work).

Everyone involved has low distress tolerance

When our trauma is triggered or our nervous systems are activated we will have very low distress tolerance. And if this has been part of our relationship for quite some time, or indeed the story of our lives, our reactivity to everyday stresses, slights and annoyances generally will be automatic. We are in a constant state of waiting – we are hypervigilant to our partners' behaviour, to them irritating us or letting us down, and we struggle to tolerate the many frustrations that are inevitable for all relationships, even healthy ones. Increasing our ability to tolerate distress so we can approach our problems in more effective ways is a key part of growth. With that in mind, having the awareness of our low distress tolerance is useful. Again, we can lose perspective by blaming our partners, believing if they simply change their behaviour our ability to cope would be better. However our partners have behaved, we can develop our distress tolerance so we are not so easily activated and reactive in unhelpful ways.

HOW TO BREAK THE PATTERN

Distress tolerance skills are a crucial part of our ability to become – and stay – secure (see page 179). Commit to increasing your ability to tolerate distress without taking it to the extremes of your anxious or avoidant ways of behaving. We have the capability to manage a difficult moment without feeling overwhelmed and stay in a constructive state of composure and equilibrium. Rather than being primed and anticipating the next upset, which keeps our nervous systems activated and our relationships hypercritical, we can learn to be more robust, to approach our problems and issues with maturity and presence of (wise) mind (see page 182).

Partners easily become emotionally dysregulated

Relationships that include anxious and avoidant individuals can be notoriously volatile. This only retraumatises all the people involved, reinforces their insecure attachment wounding and, crucially, maintains the status quo. As long as we are emotionally dysregulated it is not possible to change our behaviour. Emotional dysregulation is when we are unconscious, and when we are unconscious, nothing is going to change. In order for our relationships to work, emotional regulation needs to be viewed as an absolute priority (see Chapter 7).

HOW TO BREAK THE PATTERN

Create a strategy for managing conflict. When calm and deactivated, discuss what goes wrong when you have conflict. Examine where things start turning – remember to not be judgemental or blame, but rather be matter-of-fact and very clear. For example, 'I stop listening when you raise your voice' or 'When you go silent, I feel hurt and angry.' When we know each other's trigger points and can see where to focus our efforts, we can then utilise the communication tools laid out in Chapter 9 to manage difficult conversations more skilfully. We can also consider what works to help both partners stay in control and not return to the automatic, well-worn dance. This might be allowing a time-out so the avoidant can reflect and the anxious can de-escalate, or a safe word being used when someone realises the other has fallen into the trap, signalling it's time to stop.

Relationships are viewed in a negative way

An anxious core belief can be that relationships are unfulfilling and cause a lot of pain, and an avoidant core belief can be that relationships are overwhelming and are a source of frustration. If this is what we expect we can unconsciously create a self-fulfilling prophecy. If we fundamentally believe relationships are negative, even though we might desire something very different, we will relate to people in such a way that perpetuates this belief. Remember, the human brain seeks to recreate what it knows. We do not live our lives based on what we want; we live our lives based on what we expect and what is familiar.

HOW TO BREAK THE PATTERN

By exploring our distorted thinking (see Chapter 8) we can create a new view of relationships that is more optimistic and encouraging. If we've been hurting for a while, we may have become cynical and jaded, our view of relationships distorted with bitterness. As we take responsibility more in our partnerships, eschewing the seductive victim stance, we can also challenge ourselves to see the good in relationships and also how esteeming it is to be working on our relationships. We can shift our mindset to one that is affirming and supportive of what we're doing, which in turn will help us feel better about ourselves and relationships. This can pave the way for a more hopeful idea of love. For example, 'Relationships can be challenging sometimes. However, I am growing and learning all the time. I want the best for myself and am prepared to put in the work to achieve that.'

One or both partners struggle with empathy and compassion

When attachment trauma is triggered, there is no empathy. We can really notice when we have no empathy for our partners, where they come from, their histories and their struggles, and are lacking compassion entirely. We might also notice when we lack empathy and compassion for ourselves too. We disregard our own well-being, our histories, our fears and what we need. In a loving, healthy relationship, there is space for all this.

Bring your attention to when you feel the most empathic and compassionate towards yourself and your partner, and when that goes. This will show you the areas that need a bit more work.

Signs you're lacking in empathy and compassion

- 'Don't care' about your partner, their feelings or experience
- Can only see your own hurt and pain
- Conversely, are too preoccupied with your partner's situation and disconnected from your own/yourself

- Want to teach your partner a lesson/put them in their place
- Feel emotionally shut-down
- Are reactive and behaving recklessly or thoughtlessly
- Struggle to put yourself in your partner's shoes/see things from their perspective
- Judge or disregard their perspective

HOW TO BREAK THE PATTERN

Continue to develop the muscle of empathy and compassion, valuing your partner's perspective and feelings. The dance happens because the people involved feel so deprived of what they need (attention or space) that they cease to see themselves as a partnership, responsible for one another's happiness, and instead become self-focused and only interested in what they need as an individual. Developing and maintaining healthy levels of empathy and compassion within the relationship therefore is very important. You can do this by actively working on:

- Remembering your partner's history and where their hurts come from.
- Knowing your partner's insecurities and wanting to make them better, not worse.
- Treating each other with tenderness.
- Knowing which of your behaviours are the most hurtful to your partner and committing to not doing them/negotiating something else that is helpful.
- Taking your partner's feelings into consideration.

- Imagining how you would feel if the roles were reversed.
- Add your own: _____

If you find yourself back in the dance, recognise it as soon as possible, step away from the problem, and pivot back into the solution. Change *is* possible.

'Why is it so hard to just be nice to me?' Mackenzie would despair to partner Skylar with painful regularity. Theirs was the classic anxious avoidant relationship, with Skylar being hyper-independent and not very participative in the partnership, while Mackenzie was highly affectionate and enthusiastic about doing things together. They were both exhausted and the goodwill in the relationship was rapidly ebbing away.

Although Skylar was quite sceptical about working on their issues, when they both agreed to have more compassion for each other and focus more on making requests than arguing, they had to admit, their dynamic improved dramatically.

These shifts will make all the difference to both your experience of your relationships and the quality of your partnerships. The above suggestions can be a starting point for you and your partner, and you can add or change certain points as your relationship progresses or different issues become relevant.

The message is clear: take responsibility for both your happiness and your unhelpful behaviour; communicate respectfully with your partner as you negotiate how to take each other into account more; work on your stuff; be kind and thoughtful, and keep making goals that will improve and enhance your love.

Journalling prompts

- Which of the traps or behaviours discussed in this chapter are particularly relevant to you and your relationship?
- What have been the consequences of the anxious avoidant dance for you? Give examples.
- Are there particular steps or suggestions you think you will struggle with? Why?
- What tools from the other chapters will be important for you to utilise to relate in more secure ways?
- What specific goals would you like to set for yourself to be more secure in your relationship?

CHAPTER 12

The Avoidant Avoidant Roadblock

Partnerships between people who are predominantly avoidant can be compatible as they don't expect too much intimacy from each other, so there is a low level of disappointment in the relationship. They enjoy a lot of independence, which is important to them. They also know not to take things too personally, so therefore can have a relaxed way of communicating with each other.

People in these relationships can be very focused on things outside the relationship, which they are passionate about. That makes them very interesting people who can bring many ideas and good conversations to the relationship. They also have large lives, which again adds to the depth of the partnership, if they learn to prioritise their relationship as much as these other activities.

On the downside, these partnerships can lack chemistry and the relationships themselves can stall without commitment or a clear focus on what they want in the future. Avoiding responsibilities in life is echoed in the relationship, and the relationship can be somewhat unsatisfying and rootless.

That said, partnerships with avoidantly attached individuals can offer an unexpected opportunity for people to create unique relationship constructs that work for the people involved. Often brushing off convention, avoidantly attached individuals can embrace unconventional but satisfying relationship structures that allow for relationship connection but also individual expression and freedom. They can find what suits them and their partners, and exert significant control in their personal lives to fulfil their specific wants and needs.

The common challenges these relationships face are outlined below. Some may feel relevant to you and others may not; furthermore, there might be others not mentioned here that I hope you can adapt to the ideas laid out below to help you consider how to increase the enjoyment and longevity of the partnership.

Challenges for avoidant and avoidant relationships

- The relationship can drift as people do not invest in it.
- People are too aloof to have enough tension or chemistry to maintain a connection.
- Partners can end the relationship or walk away during conflict.
- Partners can be dismissive and hurtful.
- One partner is not intrigued by the needs of the other.
- Partners can lose control of overthinking.
- Making plans and moving forward is avoided.
- The relationship is not prioritised.
- Emotionally unavailable partners struggle with empathy and compassion.

The relationship can drift as people do not invest in it

Those with an avoidant attachment can have busy lives – with work that has great meaning to them, political or social action, exercise and fitness or creative endeavours that can take up the majority of the time. With so many passions outside the relationship that will dominate their time, avoidantly attached people can plod along in their relationships without putting in any real energy or investment. Just because people are avoidantly attached does not mean they don't wish to be in a relationship, but without the push and pull of anxious avoidant relationships, the avoidant avoidant relationship can at times be somewhat empty and neglected, due to the individuals involved being focused elsewhere.

HOW TO BREAK THE PATTERN

Invest more in the relationship. Avoidance means shying away from responsibilities, and a big responsibility we shirk is the time and effort our relationships deserve. By realising our partnerships will flourish with a little more care, we can stretch ourselves to give of ourselves and our time for the betterment of the connection. To invest more, we can look ahead and consider what we would like to achieve, or where we would like to be in five or ten years' time. Ask yourself: 'What goals would I like for the future of this relationship that would bring me pleasure and purpose? What is required from me to achieve those goals?'

People are too aloof to have enough tension or chemistry to maintain a connection

Our avoidance is about avoiding tension. Difficult conversations, conflict or emotional discussions are not our preference, so when everyone involved has an avoidant attachment, this can be a wonderful reprieve from all of that messiness. However, that also means that there aren't many ways to connect, as avoidance can be about keeping people at arm's length and we are generally quite detached from one another. Due to this, chemistry is difficult to ignite and maintain, and the relationship can suffer from a lack of connection and interest in each other.

'Otherness' can be a big part of desire, and when people relate in the same unresponsive ways it can be challenging to get the traction that attraction requires, as avoidants can be more *dis*tracted than *at*tracted.

HOW TO BREAK THE PATTERN

Make plans to do things with your partner that create connection and chemistry. It doesn't always occur to us to do something with our partners specifically or on purpose. We can change our mindset around this. It is worthwhile and useful to make time for each other, and to actively create situations where you can enjoy each other. This will help build the chemistry and connectivity that can be lacking. This could mean physical activities, outings, trips or shared interests. During this time, we can try to focus a bit more on our partners than we normally would, to remind ourselves what we like about them and to continue learning about them too.

Partners can end the relationship or walk away during conflict

When conflict does arise, people with avoidant attachment and low distress tolerance can be quick to end the relationship or not engage in difficult conversations. Those involved lack the motivation and inclination to do the work of relationships and, due to their conflict aversion and negative thinking, disagreements can be disproportionate. When partners have low investment relationships can hang in the balance. Our fear takes over and we will sooner walk away from a relationship than expose ourselves to such seemingly emotionally dangerous undertakings.

> The communication needed for conflict resolution or growth as a partnership can sometimes represent the very intimacy avoidants don't want or shy away from. This is when we can pick fights or sabotage discussions or therapy, to avoid talking through issues or being seen in the relationship.

HOW TO BREAK THE PATTERN

Work on distress tolerance so difficult conversations do not result in the relationship ending or people walking away. By utilising communication skills (see Chapter 9), we can express our internal experience and create a relationship that works for us and our partners. We can desensitise to communicating about serious subjects and realise they will not engulf us. And we can discover that in sharing our wishes with our partners, we might be able to create the relationship we want by thinking big and outside the box. Practise distress tolerance skills whenever an important conversation needs to take place, so you can withstand the initial discomfort and get the hang of sharing respectfully with your partner. Make time in your diary for such conversations (like a relationship meeting – see page 232), so they are committed to.

Partners can be dismissive and hurtful

These kinds of relationships have the capacity to hurt the people within them. When the avoidant attachment is activated, the loss of empathy facilitates making unkind statements, which can damage what little goodwill there is within the partnership.

That said, those of us with avoidant attachment can also be incredibly robust and do not take things so personally, due to our sometimes inflated self-esteem, so instead these relationships can have high levels of tolerance for disagreements, sarcasm and banter, without it being too detrimental to the partnership.

HOW TO BREAK THE PATTERN

Catch yourself being dismissive, recognise it, and reframe your thoughts to something more constructive. As outlined in Chapter 4, a trait of our avoidantly attached defence is being judgemental of others, placing ourselves in a one-up position. In order to incorporate more respect and kindness into the partnership, we need do away with destructive behaviours and make way for constructive ones in their place. See Chapter 8 for advice and strategies to reframe your thoughts. Doing a gratitude list will also help you to develop the skill of appreciation, rather than deprecation and dismissiveness.

One partner is not intrigued by the needs of the other

Avoidantly attached individuals may struggle to interest one another. Being highly detached, sometimes even dissociated, in a romantic sense, these individuals may not spark a strong attraction in one another. While they may understand one another and appreciate what is important to each other, when it comes to an emotional and physical attraction, there can be a lot that is lacking. The perfunctory nature of sex can also lead to boredom or neglecting each other physically. Having such autonomous needs and a preference to not rely on anyone else, there can be insufficient intrigue within the partnership to maintain healthy levels of desire.

HOW TO BREAK THE PATTERN

Being autonomous is useful in relationships; however, we can neglect our intimate relationship as a result. Make time every week to be close to your partner and/or have sex, if that is what you and your partner would like and it feels healthy. We can be out of touch with our intimacy needs and it might feel more comfortable ignoring or denying them. If you know it is causing problems in your relationship, it could be healthy to make time to start getting closer to your partner (unless you and your partner are content with the status quo, of course). Start off slow, like holding hands more, being affectionate, making time for each other, bathing together and holding each other in bed, without any pressure or intention of having sex. This can gently create tension and more connection.

Partners can lose control of overthinking

We can have very insular lives, a lot of it taking place in our heads as we intellectualise our life experience and relationships. We are overly rational and logical, and can be prone to overthinking or negative thinking when displeased. People in this relationship can be at the mercy of their thoughts and allow ruminating or cognitive distortions to take over, and the reality of the relationship can quickly skew in each individual's mind. Sometimes, getting lost in the freeze response, overthinking or being stuck in our heads can result in us neglecting other aspects of ourselves and each other, namely important emotional, physical and sexual needs. When logic dominates, we trample over the nuance of our relationships and each other, living in our heads rather than in the truth of our romantic partnerships.

HOW TO BREAK THE PATTERN

Make time every week to get out of your head. Being rational and logical is helpful in many areas; however, in our personal, romantic relationships it can lead to a loss of connection to ourselves (and our partners). We aren't in tune with our bodies and it would be useful to try yoga, meditation and breathwork (see page 173), visiting friends, going for walks and runs – anything to break the cycle of overthinking and intellectualising our life and relationship. Living in our heads is not the same as living in the real world, and physical activity or speaking with others can give us a break from our heads and any unhelpful thought cycles. It also lets us return to our relationships more open and engaged, de-stressed and present.

Making plans and moving forward is avoided

In our avoidance, commitment is not easy, and in a partnership where everyone is avoidant, moving the relationship forward can stall. Special life events, milestones, anniversaries and plans can all be avoided or downplayed as avoidant individuals are not comfortable with the attention such occasions can bring. Without the impetus and motivation to drive things forward, to make commitments for the future, the relationship can become somewhat hollow. Commitment is unclear and amorphous, and where the relationship is headed is not overtly discussed or agreed upon. While this may work for many people, as commitment and future planning isn't always necessary, for those individuals who do wish to start a family, share a home or have other specific goals, this lack of planning can result in dreams not being realised and windows of opportunity closing, sometimes permanently.

HOW TO BREAK THE PATTERN

Have a relationship meeting so you can consider plans for the future and commitments you wish to make (see page 232). The meeting will help you stay accountable and focused on what you are trying to achieve. It will also help you practise developing the muscle of empathy and compassion. Part of the relationship meeting is to hear your partner's perspective and take it into account. Recognise that taking other people into consideration isn't always easy for you, but you are learning to do so. It may feel effortful or even unnecessary; however, it helps mature us and remain relational. It also creates a structure around certain conversations and making plans, which helps us feel calmer and organised.

The relationship is not prioritised

Although relationships are often wanted and we can love our partners very much, actually prioritising the relationship can feel extremely challenging (or even confusing).

> For us, relationships are expected to just be, to exist on their own, without too much input, time or energy. Choosing to be in a relationship, and staying in it, can be the beginning and end of our demonstrations of commitment and effort.

Often very structured people, we are quick to get into routines and habits that do not place our relationship at the top of the list. This needn't be cause for concern if everyone is it in agreement and satisfied with what is being given.

However, it does not help us to grow and overcome some of the fear and pain that lies beneath the avoidance. We are prone to having the same projections, the same negative thinking, the same sense of alienation, because we're not doing the work of learning to be more relational.

HOW TO BREAK THE PATTERN

Write a gratitude list every week (see box below). We can be in danger of tuning out our partners, only stopping to notice things that irk or inconvenience us. This is unfair to them and creates ill-feeling in us that we then need to process. Making a gratitude list is a very easy way to break out of neglectful or negative thinking cycles and view our partners kindly; it allows them to take up a bit more positive space in our minds, too. It will help us to value our partners and also become more conscious of how our relationships enhance our life and that, without them, we would miss out on a lot. As our appreciation increases, so will our ability to prioritise our relationship.

How to make a gratitude list

Writing your list is more effective than simply doing it in your head.

- Step 1: Consider your partner. Think about what you like, find admirable, respect and think is sexy. Reflect on what they've said or done that was funny, intelligent, generous or helpful.
- Step 2: Write specific examples of what you come up with. For example:

- o 'I'm grateful my partner was understanding when I got the directions wrong.'
- o 'I'm grateful for the sexy kiss we had this morning.'
- o 'I'm grateful for my partner cooking my favourite meal tonight.'

  Write at least five points, though see if you can get to ten.
- Step 3: Try to think of new examples each time you make a gratitude list – the more specific the better. This will help continue to deepen your feelings and also nurture chemistry and interest.

Alex and Lenny had been together forever, or that's what it felt like to them anyway. Alex worked a lot and on weekends, Lenny was out most of the time doing activism work, meeting friends or taking photographs. When Lenny was with Alex, their time was spent quietly reading, arguing about bills, or going through the motions with their respective families. Alex also liked going for long walks, sometimes for hours, and then would go straight to bed after getting home. When they went away with another couple who were very affectionate and clearly having lots of sex, they felt embarrassed and realised they might need to prioritise their relationship more. They joined a gym and began doing three classes a week together. The exercise was good for them and Alex liked seeing Lenny in Lycra. This kick-started them going out to dinner every couple of weeks and enjoying critiquing the staff and the food. The spark was back.

Emotionally unavailable partners struggle with empathy and compassion

As discussed, we can intellectualise our relationships and our lives, being so overly logical and rational that the emotional part of our brain that allows us to tap in to compassion and empathy never really fires up. When our avoidant attachment is activated, we can either antagonise or shut down. Neither behaviour enables us to view our partners with kindness or care (quite the opposite) or to even think of them at all.

In order to grow as human beings and to learn more about what love is, developing our emotional understanding and empathy muscles is crucial. If we are to care for other people, we need to care about their experiences, their feelings and their point of view. We also need to learn to be gentle with others, and this is where compassion comes in.

HOW TO BREAK THE PATTERN

Nip judgement in the bud. When we are being judgemental we cannot have empathy. We need to do the hard work of imagining walking in our partners' shoes, with their history and their hurts, and to contemplate how they might be feeling about their current situation. We can have awareness of our biases and how they can limit our capacity for compassion. Rather than intellectualising and leaning too heavily on our rational minds, we can tune in to the more neglected aspects of ourselves, like emotions, so we can stay present with our loved ones and not disengage quite so easily (the emotional regulation skills in Chapter 7 help us to engage with emotions appropriately). In this way, we can bring compassion and understanding to the table and be more emotionally available.

*

Breaking our avoidant patterns may feel highly counter-intuitive, so it's important to say: you probably won't want/feel like/be inclined to challenge them. That's the point. In our avoidance, we avoid life and relationships, and thereby sabotage our chances of happy partnerships. We'd sooner have a quiet life or be on our own. If you want relationships, if you want love and to be loved, if you want a life with someone, these suggestions will help you achieve that. It's crucial we start doing things differently. Our avoidant traits and tendencies are so strong that we will default back to them very easily, so this needs our attention and our discipline. If we want a different kind of future, these are some of the steps we can take.

Journalling prompts

- Which of the traps or behaviours discussed in this chapter are particularly relevant to you and your relationship?
- What have been the consequences of the avoidant avoidant roadblock for you? Give examples.
- Are there particular steps or suggestions you think you will struggle with? Why?
- What tools from the other chapters will be important for you to utilise to relate in more secure ways?
- What specific goals would you like to set for yourself to be more secure in your relationship?

CHAPTER 13

The Anxious Anxious Fusion

O n the face of it, you might imagine that more than one anxiously attached person in a relationship would be just too much emotion to handle. In reality, anxiously attached people who join to form relationships can create harmonious partnerships as they understand each other's needs and are inclined to meet them.

Although the initial attraction might be somewhat thwarted, without a more avoidant dynamic with which to gain traction, over time, anxiously attached partnerships can enjoy more contentment and peace than the overt chemistry of anxious avoidance romances. Their relationship can feel intense and quite high-maintenance; however, each partner is all too happy to put in the effort. Because of the high-functioning nature of everyone involved, this relationship can be very rich, full, productive and close.

On the downside, people in these relationships can become enmeshed, without exercising enough independence. Their relationship can become the focus of their lives, thereby creating imbalance and disproportion with outside life. Because anxiously attached people fall in love easily, these relationships can progress very quickly, sometimes too quickly. Partners may not take the time to truly get to know each other and discover if they have compatible goals, values, temperaments and personalities, which can cause significant distress down the line.

Also, anxiety is contagious. If we are around someone with a degree of angst and we are of a susceptible and sensitive constitution, we can easily become angsty ourselves.

Emotional regulation (see Chapter 7) will be very important to the health and well-being of this relationship, because without it, everyday difficulty can become escalated, and difficult conversations are either left unresolved or are sources of conflict and disconnect. Learning to communicate calmly and constructively (see Chapter 9) will be a useful focus, as will having boundaries around tone of voice, language, venting and complaining.

The common challenges these relationships face are outlined below. Not all of these may feel relevant to you or I may have left out some that you experience. I hope you can reflect on the ideas I've suggested and can strengthen the resilience of your partnership and begin to feel more secure.

Challenges for anxious and anxious relationships

- Due to dependency needs, the relationship becomes enmeshed.
- High levels of anxiety cause needs to go unspoken and unacknowledged.
- There is an over-focus on the relationship and outside life is neglected.
- Mutual fear becomes normalised.
- The relationship becomes high-conflict with frequent arguments.

- Partners become easily emotionally dysregulated, venting uncontrollably.
- There is too much focus on emotions and problems, and not enough on making plans and moving forward. OR things move too fast, without a strong enough foundation.

Due to dependency needs, the relationship becomes enmeshed

While an avoidant avoidant relationship can be too outward-looking, the anxious anxious partnership can be too inward-looking: we can be overly focused on the other person and dependent on them for our own well-being and equilibrium. When individuals who are anxiously attached come together, they can become enmeshed and over-involved in each other's lives, unsure where one person ends and the other begins.

Interdependence is what we're all aiming for in our partnerships: needing each other but also able to meet our own needs. Those in anxious anxious relationships can surrender their autonomy too easily and co-dependently rely on each other in extreme, imbalanced and unhealthy ways.

HOW TO BREAK THE PATTERN

The challenge is to maintain a degree of independence while also enjoying the closeness of this kind of relationship. We do this by holding on to a sense of individuality and agency on our own, prioritising our self-care (see page 158), having boundaries so we don't become overly dependent (see Chapter 10), and maintaining a strong sense of responsibility for oneself.

Dependent

- constant need to be together all the time
- isolate self from others outside the relationship
- doesn't have any boundaries
- looks to the other person to rescue or fix
- learnt helplessness (see page 156)
- constant and unhealthy need for reassurance
- profound fears of rejection/losing love
- conflict-averse or high-conflict
- knows more about others' emotions than their own

Independent

- enjoys time together and on one's own
- enjoys the company of others outside the relation-ship
- has boundaries and feels confident
- looks to others for support as takes responsibility for self
- accountable
- appreciates reassurance and feels secure
- values relationships and love
- can communicate and deal with difficulty
- does self-work to understand their emotions

High levels of anxiety cause needs to go unspoken and unacknowledged

Most of us with anxious attachment may feel we are expressing ourselves most of the time; however, often our communication is not direct and clear. We can be disconnected from our needs, losing sight of them, and complaining or nagging instead. Due to high levels of anxiety and emotionality, and a propensity towards disappointment, we can be reticent to speak up and be honest with our partners for fear of rejection, which is so familiar to us. In this way, a lot of our needs can go unacknowledged by both ourselves and our partners because we are disconnected from that part of us and we try to hide those vulnerable aspects of ourselves. We may crave our partners' connection, closeness and attention, but are not aware of the deeper needs beneath.

HOW TO BREAK THE PATTERN

Having needs is human, and we can take time and care to connect with our needs, otherwise our anxiety can get in the way and divert away from our wishes. Anxiety management is crucial, as we can become fixated on alleviating our anxiety rather than meeting our core needs. For example: we can want our partners to come home early from a night out (to appease our anxiety) rather than strengthening our robustness and working on our trust within ourselves and the relationship (to meet our core security needs).

Managing the anxiety, by regulating and co-regulating (see page 174), to maintain a calm equilibrium will transform everyone in this partnership, healing many wounds. Communication skills also need to be developed and worked on every day (see Chapter 9).

There is an over-focus on the relationship and outside life is neglected

We will prioritise our relationships over everything else. And while this is appropriate in many regards, it can become imbalanced, as we neglect other aspects of our life, allowing our partners and relationships to be our only real source of connection and well-being. Our careers can be sidelined, hobbies abandoned and projects forgotten about because all our time and energy is spent on our partners and relationships. This is a natural part of certain stages of the relationship, particularly the beginning; however, this can become the staple of the relationship and we can lose sight of our greater lives, as we are over-invested in our relationships to the point where it's almost as if nothing else exists.

HOW TO BREAK THE PATTERN

Each person keeps their life big, spending plenty of time on career, hobbies, passions, other friends, activities and social events. In order to keep the relationship expansive and healthy, we can maintain an active social life and the aspects of our lives that were present before meeting our partners. When we are anxiously attached we are prone to losing ourselves in our relationships, so by staying plugged in to our own lives, friendships and support systems, we can stay grounded in our sense of self and keep our lives big and beautiful.

Mason and Jenny finished each other's sentences and did everything together. None of which was a problem – until Jenny's promotion required her to work longer hours and sometimes travel. Left with more time on his hands, Mason realised that, without Jenny, his life was very small. The highlight of his day was when they would FaceTime but because of the time difference when she travelled, even that often didn't happen. He began to feel depressed and pined for her whenever she worked late or was away.

They both realised they had become too dependent on each other and needed to do things differently. Slowly, Mason got back in touch with old friends and started playing the guitar again. Jenny enjoyed her work and loved catching up with Mason when she got back. Having more going on outside the relationship reignited their sex life and they had lots more to talk about. They realised balance was healthy and they were happier as a result.

Mutual fear becomes normalised

Anxiety is about fear, and our greatest fear is to be rejected or abandoned, so our need for proximity and reassurance can be all-encompassing. Our fears can take over and, when everyone involved is fearful and anxious, it can become an unhealthy part of the home environment. Being highly fear-based, instead of sharing love and care with one another, we can instead trade fearful projections and worry, and maintain the high level of anxiety that is part of this kind of partnership. In an ideal world, anxious people are able to soothe one another's fears so they can become more secure. However, in a less healthy dynamic, anxious people maintain and exacerbate each partner's anxieties. Together, the anxiety gets further entrenched, not less.

HOW TO BREAK THE PATTERN

Focus on courage, so fears can be challenged and the anxiety is kept at bay. Within most anxiously attached individuals lies a huge amount of determination. People with anxious attachment desire love deeply and are prepared to go to any lengths to get it. Therefore, people in a relationship who are anxiously attached can endeavour to bring out the best in each other, tackling their problems with bravery and dedication. This can be one of the great joys of this romantic partnership.

The relationship becomes high-conflict with frequent arguments

Sadly, volatile interactions can be a big part of our history, which we will bring with us into these partnerships. Having people who are familiar with high-conflict ways of relating can be unhelpful when we are trying to be more secure. Calm conversations are not what we are accustomed to; instead, we turn minor issues into arguments, sometimes escalating difficulty into painful conflict and repetitive rows. We might also enjoy the passion and possible high that can come from high-conflict altercations, gaining reassurance from our partners that they care for us through their ability to fight with us. None of this is healthy and resentment will continue to build until ambivalence inevitably strikes, when even more suffering will ensue.

HOW TO BREAK THE PATTERN

Boundaries can be utilised here and are supremely helpful in many regards:

- We can analyse our arguments and see where we take a wrong turn.
- We can set boundaries for ourselves for when and where and for how long we have difficult conversations.
- We can set time limits to avoid conversations escalating and becoming destructive.

- We can have boundaries around our tone of voice and the language we use, so we stay respectful and also honest with each other.

See Chapter 10 for more strategies on creating boundaries in your life.

Partners become easily emotionally dysregulated, venting uncontrollably

When anxious, we can have a hair-trigger response. It is very easy for us to become emotionally dysregulated because our anxiety is always ticking over, waiting for the next episode. We can fall into the trap of venting to our partners in uncontained and destructive ways, which maintains the destructive nature of interactions and can make feeling secure unlikely. Secure attachment is about having a regulated nervous system and, for those of us with anxiety, dysregulated nervous systems are what we unconsciously perpetuate (see page 49). As we are sensitive people whose emotions will generally be in charge of us, emotional regulation will need to be a priority for this kind of relationship, otherwise the anxiously attached relating patterns will continue forevermore.

HOW TO BREAK THE PATTERN

Make emotionally regulating exercises part of your daily life (see Chapter 7). Having a nervous system that is accustomed to becoming activated in an instant, or is activated permanently, will block the growth in this relationship. But maintaining a deactivated nervous system will create the cushion required when difficult circumstances present themselves and allow new behaviours and ways of relating to develop. Find what works for you: breathwork, meditation, mindfulness, visualisations, exercise ... There are many tools we can use to de-stress our bodies as well as many forms of therapy. We also need to have boundaries in place to take responsibility for our venting and emotional dumping.

Finally, examine other factors that may be keeping your body stressed. Are your hormones balanced? Do you get enough sleep? How is your work/life balance? How much caffeine do you consume? Do you drink and take drugs to excess? Do you eat unhealthily? All of these either provide or deprive us of what we need to keep our bodies and minds stable and able to cope with whatever life throws at us.

There is too much focus on emotions and problems, and not enough on making plans and moving forward. OR things move too fast, without a strong enough foundation

Just as the avoidant avoidant relationships can be too rational and logical, without any real emotional connection driving the relationship forward, so too the anxious anxious relationship can be too emotive and fear-based to make concrete plans and trust that the relationship will progress. We can hold ourselves back through the ongoing arguments within the partnership, focusing on minor and often irrelevant details or issues, which helps this partnership avoid looking at bigger and more important issues and choosing future goals. We spend our lives spinning our wheels in the day-to-day anxieties, never allowing ourselves to look further down the road than our latest drama or upset.

On the other hand, these partnerships can establish very

quickly, as those involved fall in love with incredible speed, moving things on too soon. In our desire for security, and for all our hopes and dreams to come true, we can embark on whirlwind relationships where we are quick to commit, make massive life decisions and alter the trajectory of our lives. We may not take the time to really get to know one another, to build a strong foundation and to ascertain if our goals and personalities are compatible – not just in the short term, but the medium and long term too. We can feel too fearful to not commit immediately, wanting to get the security and guarantees as quickly as possible, without allowing time to understand what is on offer, what everyone could expect, the nature of a life together, and if it is likely to help us feel content, secure and fulfilled.

HOW TO BREAK THE PATTERN

In early relationships, take things slow. Give yourselves the gift of time. The beginning phases of romantic relationships are particularly excruciating for people with anxious attachment. The insecurity of not knowing whether things will work out, whether the person likes us, whether we are meant to be together can be overwhelming. We want to save ourselves from this agony as quickly as possible, and that is why we can get committed to people very quickly.

Craving a love story, we can fall for people very quickly and very hard, but without really knowing them well enough, ignoring personality incompatibilities and clashing temperaments.

Taking time, slowing things down and having boundaries around how often you see each other, how much you message each other and how soon you have sex will all help you and your nervous system make the best and healthiest choices for yourself moving forward.

If in an established relationship, have medium-to-long-term plans that are agreed upon to give the relationship purpose and meaning. In both a high-conflict and a conflict-averse relational dynamic, we can lose sight of what we want, both now and in the future. We can hold ourselves back from saying what we want or agree too easily to things that may not be right for us. By maintaining good communication (see Chapter 9), we can continue to explore the bigger picture of the relationship. By committing to a regular relationship meeting (page 232), we can have very clear goals we are working towards within our relationships, both to keep the relationship healthy and to make defined plans for our future, so everybody can stay on track and keep focused on the prize – a long-term, satisfying life and relationship.

There can be a lot of hope with this partnership. The people involved are often motivated to do the work and can bring great sensitivity and compassion to the relationship. The biggest stumbling block is the level of anxiety each party brings. Anxiety can be voracious, and it can sometimes be insatiable and destructive if we cannot manage it well over the long term. By following the suggestions above, and troubleshooting difficulties as they arise, you can begin to experience relationships through a more secure lens. You can recognise the difference between anxiety and security, and you can see the impact each has on your well-being and relationship. Secure attachment is nervous system work and, in this partnership, that needs to be the cornerstone of all that you do. By creating safety for yourself and your partner, you can heal in profoundly powerful ways.

Journalling prompts

- Which of the traps or behaviours discussed in this chapter are particularly relevant to you and your relationship?
- What have been the consequences of the anxious anxious fusion for you? Give examples.
- Are there particular steps or suggestions you think you will struggle with? Why?
- What tools from the other chapters will be important for you to utilise to relate in more secure ways?
- What specific goals would you like to set for yourself to be more secure in your relationship?

CHAPTER 14

The Secure Insecure Opportunity

Having discussed the different combinations of possible relationships, I want to conclude by reflecting on what could be possible if we (as insecure people) have a relationship with someone secure or we do the work to become more secure and our partners don't, so they remain insecure. Sometimes secure insecure partnerships offer a significant opportunity:

- There is good chemistry as both are intrigued by the other.
- The needs of one challenge the other to grow and mature.
- The person who is insecure may heal within a safe, nurturing relationship.
- Conflict and emotional dysregulation fail to escalate due to the secure person's lack of reactivity.
- The insecure party grows a new view of relationships as positive and calming.
- Empathy and compassion is modelled in the relationship.
- Trauma response can be tended to and the relationship status quo is supportive and non-triggering.

Being with someone secure, or even someone working on being secure, presents a real chance for us to find a safe place and secure bliss. When insecure people come together, the only knowledge they have is of relating in ways that are sadly rooted in perpetuating their insecure attachment. When engaging with someone who is secure, we are shown something different – a new possibility. We cannot get the same rise from someone who is secure and, therefore, the high-conflict or reactive ways of relating we are accustomed to are replaced with a more genuine desire to problem-solve, soothe and create harmony. These kinds of relationships can truly repair insecure hurts, teaching us that relationships are both sustaining and nurturing.

People who are securely attached can also learn a lot from those with insecure attachment, as they will help them understand complexity and they can develop greater levels of compassion. Both are also invited to harness specific communication skills, taking other people into account and learning how to have difficult conversations. The secure individual may have to go a little bit deeper than they are perhaps accustomed to, which will emotionally and psychologically wisen them and their understanding of themselves and others.

We must, however, also take into account what can happen when that possibility is not realised – when the relationship collapses under the weight of incompatibility and imbalance. Because this is what can and does happen to many relationships.

When only one person is secure, or is working towards being secure, there is no guarantee of things ending happily ever after. Our behaviour can certainly change the dynamics of relationships, and we can become healthier, happier people within our partnerships, regardless of what our partners are doing. However, if there is grave insecurity within the partnership, and the other person is not willing to work on it, this can end up having big implications for people who are secure.

> Not having enough experience or familiarity with certain kinds of dysfunctional ways of relating, a secure person can be wrong-footed and not recognise red flags or problematic behaviour due to their inherent trust in the goodwill of others.

Over time, a secure person can become insecure themselves, as they take on the shape and functioning of their relational environment. Either becoming anxious or avoidant themselves as a way of coping, they too retreat into a defensive stance and the relationship becomes insecure. They are then prone to falling into all the traits, tendencies and relationship patterns explored in this book.

This is an important consequence to be aware of as it is based on who we choose to have in our lives. Working on our relationships is always possible, and we want to be growing throughout our lives, but who we choose to be with and what is on offer with the people we are with must be prioritised if we are to have the relationships we wish for.

When we are secure, we no longer operate on such a primitive level. We can therefore become susceptible to other people's defensive ways of being and how they protect themselves can hurt us. So while there is much possibility in the insecure secure relationship, there is also the probability of pain and difficulty if the appropriate work and growth is not taking place. This is a hard truth we need to see and accept. We need to always have our hearts *and* our eyes open when assessing our relationships, making sure we are not staying in relationships that ultimately are not right for us.

How Hard Is Too Hard?

Sometimes, we can remain too long in unhealthy relationships, ignoring incompatibilities and our declining mental and emotional health. So feeling clear on where to invest our energy (and hearts) is a very sobering part of our work. On the other hand, however, we can also end promising relationships prematurely, without putting in the necessary efforts to grow, evolve and see what's possible.

We can get confused about when we need to stay in relationships and keep working on them and when we need to end the relationship as we've gone as far as we can go with this person. Not all relationships are *meant* to go the distance. Sometimes we hold on for too long and other times we throw in the towel too early. It's difficult to judge it correctly, especially when our emotions and stories get involved and muddy the waters.

Signs your relationship is not viable

There are challenges in every relationship. Learning to grow together can be the great gift of our partnerships. However, it's important to recognise when what's happening within a relationship is neither healthy nor sustainable. We need to look after our well-being at all times, and that means acknowledging when things are just too hard and it's time to walk away.

- They lack any insight into their unhelpful behaviour.
- They are ambivalent about you and their insecure attachment makes them totally unreachable.
- The relationship is stuck, not moving forward and not a lot of fun, either.

- You are scared to be honest and walk on eggshells a lot of the time.
- They actively push you away, are shut-down, and aren't interested in you or your feelings/needs.
- Sex is the only time you truly connect but it doesn't feel secure or relaxed. Or sex and intimacy don't feature in your relationship at all (and this is not discussed).
- They are active addicts or have mental health issues for which they resist (genuine) treatment.
- They have no desire to work on their stuff or grow (and are rude about people who do want to work on themselves).
- The relationship is dramatic and high-conflict and you're addicted to it.
- You cannot be yourself with the other person or you don't like who you are when you're with the other person.
- Destructive behaviour like shouting, name-calling and emotional abuse has become normalised.
- They struggle to communicate and dodge serious conversations.

Should you stay together for the kids?

As you've discovered in this book, part of how we learn how to have relationships is from the relationship our parents/caregivers have with each other – and your children will do the same. They will be watching how you speak to each other, the attitudes you have towards each other, how affectionate you are, how kind (or unkind) you are, how much supportiveness is evident, how fun or playful you are together, and they will even intuit how often you have sex. They will learn it all. This will be unconsciously transmitted into their attachment systems and becomes their blueprint for relationships they will go on to engage in.

With that in mind, we can ask ourselves these questions: What am I showing/teaching my child(ren) about love and relationships? Would I be happy with my child being in the kind of relationship I am modelling for them (unhappy, unhealthy, strained, loveless, sexless, and so on)?

If you and your partner are working on your relationship, then that's a wonderful example to your children. You're teaching time, effort, problem-solving and commitment in the name of love.

However, if you are stuck and the above list applies to you, you may wish to consider offering your children another option: contentment and health on one's own or the chance at/belief in a happier, healthier kind of love with someone else.

Behaviour to never ignore

- abuse (mental, emotional and physical)
- lying and deceit
- manipulative behaviour
- anger management issues
- controlling behaviour

If these are evident in your partner, seek professional help and the support of loved ones to get out of this dangerous situation.

Signs a Relationship Is Worth Working On

Relationships can be rich with possibility or they can be an emotional dead end. Many people in long-term, happy partnerships will talk about sticking it out and never giving up, and there's great wisdom to this attitude. If we're with people who are kind, decent and respectful, and who we're able to grow with, however slowly, then the possibilities are endless. But we need to be very discerning about who we choose and find out if they are able to walk that road with us.

Here are some things to consider that show our relationships are worth working on some more and our partners could be a good choice.

They are fundamentally kind, decent people

I always say to my clients – this is the starting point. If you know in your heart that you are dealing with a fundamentally good person then, I assure you, that really is enough at first. It's when we ignore narcissistic tendencies, emotionally abusive behaviour, anger issues and serious mental health conditions that the person is not prepared to take responsibility for that we are sabotaging our chances of genuine security and happiness.

They know they have some unhelpful behaviours

No one is perfect, least of all ourselves. If your partner is able to recognise that they do things that aren't helpful in the relationship, that they have their own baggage and that relationships often require effort, then you really have something to work with. This is something that can be developed together.

They seem to care about you even if they struggle to show it

Pay attention to how someone treats you. We don't express or demonstrate love in the same ways. Some people might struggle to express themselves, they may need more time on their own, and they might still be learning when it comes to praising or being affectionate to their loved ones. However, if they care about you, and this is demonstrated in their behaviour through acts of service, reliability or life admin, then you might be on to a winner, you just need to see it.

There is basic respect all the time

If you have kids, or if you are planning to have kids, this is a good test. Is the way you speak to each other and treat each other good enough to do in front of little people? Respect is a surprisingly difficult thing to maintain in our relationships all the time. It's easy to become irritated and dismissive, belittling or rude. Asking ourselves if our partners' behaviour, and our own, would serve as a good example to our children can give us the perspective we need. Remembering our dignity and maintaining healthy boundaries (see Chapter 10) helps us to keep respect as the baseline of our relationship.

They are open to working on themselves

Many people still feel that asking for help represents a failure. We have been conditioned from a very young age to deal with our problems alone and this can create a big disconnect in our relationships, which by definition need to grow and develop. So having a partner who is open to working on themselves shows amazing promise for our future with them.

Calm and loving moments are possible

Security comes from having a calm nervous system when we are with our partners. High-conflict couples struggle with this. If drama and walking on eggshells is the norm for your relationship, that is not a good sign. However, if you are able to have calm and loving moments, these are what need to be developed and nurtured. It shows that it is possible to have security with this person. A commitment needs to be made to step away from the high-conflict processes and instead to make as much space as possible for – and to prioritise – these calm, loving moments.

They are in therapy or addiction recovery

People who are in therapy doing the work are rock stars. They deserve our respect and admiration for this. Denial is a huge part of any issue, so finally accepting the need for help is a huge achievement for anyone. People who are in therapy and addiction recovery not only show that they are able to take responsibility for their stuff but also that they are committed to working on something in the long term. If they are serious about their personal work, this is someone you can build something with.

You can be totally yourself with them

I often say being relaxed is the same as being happy. In our increasingly tense and stressed lives, being truly relaxed is something we are experiencing less and less. And that is especially true in our relationships, where we can be very self-conscious and on edge. If we sense we can't be who we are, our behaviour will change and we can become hyper-vigilant, lack spontaneity and worry about other people's reactions to us. Prioritising self-care (self-soothing, boundaries and being secure in relationships) allows us to relax into who we are and can guide us to whether we can in fact be ourselves in the relationship . . . and if it's viable for us and our future.

You can speak freely and openly

Many of us were raised in families where what we thought wasn't really taken into account. We weren't encouraged to have a voice and speak up. And if we dared, we were quickly told to keep quiet or that we didn't know what we were talking about. Sometimes these feelings and themes can be echoed in our adult relationships, and we lose our voice and censor ourselves. If you can speak openly in your relationship now, that is fantastic. Open communication shows growth is definitely possible.

The grass is always greener . . .

Is it true that it's easier to leave our relationships than work on them? Looking at our own behaviour and growing our relationships is no walk in the park. It requires willingness and strength, and a large dose of humility, which can swiftly exhaust many people. In a world of online dating, matchmaking apps and services, there is a seeming abundance of 'other people who would be better'.

We look at people in relationships and judge how we feel on the inside with what they're projecting on the outside. We imagine it's easier for others and it should be easy for us too. We are tired of all this difficulty and we're tired of the hard work that we do.

The grass may be greener elsewhere but if we tend to our grass in more intentional and impactful ways, we might be surprised by how lovely our lawn can be.

Journalling prompts

- Can you ascertain whether your relationship is viable or not and whether you think that, with work, it could become more secure?
- Which of the viable/unviable lists are relevant to you and your current situation?
- What feelings came up for you when reading this chapter and why?
- Is it hard for you to let go of unhealthy relationships or can you leave relationships too soon?
- Finally, take some time and describe your life as you envisage having a secure, loving, calm relationship. Really imagine what this looks and feels like, what is happening within yourself and in your life, and how this will impact your mental, emotional and spiritual health. *That's* what this work is for!

Conclusion: It's Worth It

Now that you have finished this book, I want you to return to it often. We need constant reminding because, left to our own devices, we will shift back to old ways of behaving and insecure ways of relating very quickly. We need to bring self-awareness to our relationships every day, and know ourselves and our partners.

Life can be so stressful, and that stress will land on our relationship unless we are paying attention. How we deal with it is what's going to make all the difference. Insecurely attached relating styles come out in times of stress, relationship difficulty, or when we are experiencing a trying phase. This is part of life but, by practising with the tools in this book, we can arrive at these challenging times with clarity, allowing love and courage to guide us every step of the way.

As we learn about relationships and how to get to know other people better, we do the same for ourselves. Who are we? What do we stand for? What do we value? What do we want out of life? If we answer these questions honestly, we will see that our insecure attachment behaviours will get in the way of achieving these. I hope you are clearer now about the areas that require your attention, and that you've learnt about yourself, your needs, hopes and your dreams. Because they matter.

This book has been about love. Love is an action. Love is often an effort. Love is not something we hope we feel – it is a decision we make every day. By learning how to demonstrate love, to understand the difference between love and fear, we have the capacity to heal not only ourselves but often our partners and children too.

Developing new behaviour is a daily, conscious effort and intention. Commit to moving away from your attachment comfort zone and stretch yourself to behave in more secure ways. Remember, our insecure attachment is self-fulfilling: what we 'want' to do is what maintains the status quo. We need to actively incorporate more secure behaviour into our lives and relationships so healthy change can take place. Nothing changes if nothing changes.

Having learnt about your attachment style(s), how to break your insecure relating patterns (both anxious and avoidant), and the traps we can fall into, let's now consolidate the behaviour you worked on in your journalling questions to create goals you can commit to in order to grow and become secure and happy in your partnerships.

By setting goals, you can stay focused, so you can grow and not get stuck staring at the problem. It's so helpful to have goals we are working on in our relationships. They not only give us direction and focus, they can also help us cut through the noise of our defences or fears and stay in the reality of what we're trying to achieve. For example, having a goal of sending your partner one loving text a day isn't about whether you have time, anything to say or if they 'deserve it'; it's a goal that you can simply do that will help your relationship. Anxiety and avoidance is about focusing on the problems; being secure is about focusing on simple solutions that create a happy, harmonious relationship.

A great way to set goals is to discuss them with your partner. What would mean a lot to them? What would help their needs be met more? What simple, achievable steps can be made to improve your day-to-day lives together?

Great goals to have could be:

- Letting my partner finish speaking, and concentrating on listening.
- Doing distress tolerance and emotion-regulating exercises every day.
- Keeping my tone of voice calm and respectful.
- Making specific, direct requests and noticing when I'm complaining.
- Spending __ minutes a day totally focused on my partner, connecting with them.
- Asking for reassurance and choosing to believe the words.
- Having sex every week (if that feels healthy).

Regularly reading sections of this book will keep you moving in the right direction. You can apply the tools to different parts of your life and different difficulties that appear in your relationship. They can be utilised over and over, and each time it will improve your relational skills and deepen your wisdom and understanding.

If you are able to do this, after a period of time, something remarkable will happen to you. You'll start to feel calmer. You will feel lighter. You will see the power you have and you will use that power all the time. This will develop your self-esteem and you'll notice you feel better about yourself. You will state your needs simply and directly. Your boundaries will hold you steady and you'll like who you are in the partnership. You will be surprised how changes in you impact your partner. You won't be so easily riled up or so easily hurt, and when you are you'll share it with your partner and connect *because* of it. You will be philosophical and grounded, and probably give great advice to your friends. Your relationship will not be such a struggle because you will experience peace and ease. Your fears will subside.

You'll be in love.

Recommended Reading

Amen, Daniel G., *You, Happier* (Tyndale House, 2022)

Beck, Aaron, *Cognitive Therapy and the Emotional Disorders* (Penguin, 1991)

Beck, Judith S., *Cognitive Behavior Therapy: Basics and Beyond*, 3rd edn (Guilford Press, 2020)

Bowlby, John, *A Secure Base: Clinical Applications of Attachment Theory*, (Routledge, 2005)

Bowlby, John, *The Making and Breaking of Affectional Bonds* (Routledge, 2005)

Bray, Suzette, *DBT Explained* (Rockridge Press, 2022)

Brown, Brené, *The Power of Vulnerability* audiobook (Sounds True Inc., 2015)

Cotton, Fearne, *Calm* (Orion, 2018)

Dobelli, Rolf, *The Art of Thinking Clearly* (Hodder & Stoughton, 2014)

Dryden, Windy, *Think Your Way to Happiness* (Sheldon Press, 1990)

Ellis, Albert, *How to Stubbornly Refuse to Make Yourself Miserable* (Robinson, 2019)

Gottman, John and Gottman, Julie Schwartz, *Fight Right: How Successful Couples Turn Conflict into Connection* (Penguin Life, 2024)

Heller, Diane Poole, *The Power of Attachment* (Sounds True Inc., 2019)

Kuburic, Sara, *It's On Me* (Quercus, 2023)

Linehan, Marsha M., *DBT Skills Training Handouts and Worksheets* (Guilford Press, 2014)

Perel, Esther, *Mating in Captivity* (Hodder and Stoughton, 2007)

Rosellini, Gayle and Worden, Mark, *Of Course You're Angry: A Guide to Dealing with the Emotion of Substance Abuse*, 2nd edn (Hazelden Trade, 2018)

Rosenberg, Marshall B., *Nonviolent Communication: A Language of Life*, 3rd edn (Puddle Dancer Press, 2015)

Schwartz, Richard C. and Sweezy, Martha, *Internal Family Systems Therapy*, 2nd edn (Guilford Press, 2019)

Shetty, Jay, *8 Rules of Love* (Thorsons, 2023)

Smith, Julie, *Why Has Nobody Told Me This Before?* (Michael Joseph, 2022)

Tawwab, Nedra Glover, *Set Boundaries, Find Peace: A Guide to Reclaiming Yourself* (Piatkus, 2021)

Wegscheider-Cruse, Sharon, *Another Chance: Hope and Health for the Alcoholic Family*, 2nd edn (Science and Behavior Books, 1990)

Wiest, Brianna, *101 Essays That Will Change the Way You Think* (Thought Catalog Books, 2018)

Acknowledgements

I would like to thank my clients. I always boast I have the best clients, which is ludicrous, I know (but it's true). There aren't many careers in which you can enjoy deeply meaningful relationships with people as you accompany them on their gravest challenges and, therefore, some of the most important and defining moments of their life. I love my work and I am so grateful to my clients who have let me into their world.

Eternal thanks must go to the greatest teachers of my life: my two stepsons. I met them when I was 29 and quite early in my career, and they truly taught me the art of love. They showed me how trust is built, how to have integrity, how important it is to tell the truth, and to not be reckless with another human's emotions. They cracked open my heart and I will be forever indebted to them for their vulnerability, joyfulness and irreverent, razor-sharp banter.

Thank you to Liz Connor who first approached me about writing this book. That was a good day. Thank you for valuing my work and imagining it in book form.

Thank you so much to my editor, Julia Kellaway, who, with great wisdom and skill, whipped this book into shape and held a steady, sure vision for what it could be. Many thanks also to Liz Marvin and Alice Brett.

Thank you to everyone at Ebury and Vermilion, and especial thanks to former publishing director Susanna Abbott and senior editor Anya Hayes, who were kind and patient from the beginning, and allowed me to get all the support I needed from start to finish.

An important mention for my wonderful supervisor, Dr Karin Dorell. Another key relationship, Karin and I have worked together for well over 17 years. Being a supervisor is very similar to being a mentor, and I'm incredibly fortunate to have benefited from her expertise and embodiment of secure attachment. Thank you also for being an early reader of this book, supporting me as you always do, bringing clarity to my instinctive way of working.

I am so deeply grateful to my best friend Janey, who was an unerring cheerleader from the moment this book was even hinted at. My greatest champion and dearest soulmate, thank you for your unconditional love. Your friendship is cherished.

Thank you also to my wonderful colleague Lauren, who commiserated with me during this creative process and who kept my spirits up with humour and unrelenting optimism.

So much appreciation to my therapist, John Beveridge, for the consistency and care over so many years. For the secure base, the quiet calm and the status-quo-challenging interventions. Heartfelt gratitude also to relationship coach Susan Quilliam, whose huge wisdom and generosity of spirit guided my husband and me through some very challenging, choppy waters and who taught us how to fly in formation.

There was a lot of death in my family during the writing of this book. My sister-in-law was the first dreadful loss, leaving us much too soon and unexpectedly. Six months later, it was my father, the man who instilled in me an insatiable love of books, and therefore writing. It is a personal tragedy that he will never be able to read my own. Four months after my father died, my father-in-law left us too, himself a writer of ten brilliant books. Finally, during the editing of this manuscript, my mother-in-law passed away, leaving a huge heart-shaped hole in the family fabric. With all this bereavement, I was convinced I would be too grief-stricken to keep writing but found quite the contrary: I felt compelled and driven to write a book that is ultimately about love. Loving as best we can, while we can. As we say in the therapy world (and as all John Bowlby's books on attachment attest), you can't talk about love without talking about loss. And so, the book took on yet another layer for me.

Special thanks to my mother for housing and feeding me, and babysitting my beloved mini sausage dog, at various stages during the (sometimes hellish) task of meeting deadlines. You juggled family, grief, obligations, home life and all the Sod's law imaginable with grace and grit.

Thanks also to my brothers for their rallying and enthusiasm, their long lunches (and longer dinners) and their encouragement of the new author in the family.

Many thanks to my husband's sister, who, despite her own bereavement, maintained nothing but kindness for me and my work, and to both my sisters-in-law who have always treated me like family.

Finally, thank you to my husband. My rock, my dreamer, my safe place. I love you with my whole heart, and every day it just gets better.

About the Author

Charisse Cooke is an attachment-based psychotherapist. She has built a dynamic Instagram community where she shares practical tools and strategies to help us develop healthy, stable and secure bonds with those we love.

You can find her on Instagram @charissecooke, TikTok @charissecookeofficial and www.charissecooke.com

Index

Note: page numbers in **bold** refer to diagrams.